Making TEDDY BEARS

Kooler Design Studio, Inc.
399 Taylor Blvd. Suite 104
Pleasant Hill, CA. 94523

Making TEDDY BEARS

CELEBRATING 100 YEARS

PROJECTS ▪ PATTERNS ▪ HISTORY ▪ LORE

PAIGE GILCHRIST

LARK BOOKS

A Division of Sterling Publishing Co., Inc.
New York

Editor: PAIGE GILCHRIST

Art Director: DANA IRWIN

Photographer: SANDRA STAMBAUGH

Pattern Designer & Consultant: BETH HILL

Assistant Editors: VERONIKA ALICE GUNTER, HEATHER SMITH, AND CATHARINE SUTHERLAND

Editorial Assistant: RAIN NEWCOMB

Assistant Art Director: HANNES CHAREN

Illustrator: ORRIN LUNDGREN

"Illustration" by E.H. Shepard, from WINNIE-THE-POOH by A. A. Milne, illustrated by E. H. Shepard, copyright 1926 by E. P. Dutton, renewed 1954 by A. A. Milne. Used by permission of Dutton Children's Books, an imprint of Penguin Putnam Books for Young Readers, a division of Penguin Putnam Inc. Line illustration by E.H. Shepard copyright under the Berne Convention, reproduced by permission of Curtis Brown Ltd., London.

Library of Congress Cataloging-in-Publication Data

Gilchrist, Paige.
    Making teddy bears : celebrating 100 years : projects, patterns, history, lore / by Paige Gilchrist.
      p. cm.
    Includes index.
    ISBN 1-57990-240-5 (hbk.) 1-57990-379-7 (pbk.)
    1. Teddy bears. 2. Soft toy making. I. Title.

TT174.3 .G55 2001
745.592'43—dc21

00-140133

10 9 8 7 6 5 4 3 2 1

Published by Lark Books, a division of
Sterling Publishing Co., Inc.
387 Park Avenue South, New York, N.Y. 10016

First Paperback Edition 2002
© 2001, Lark Books

Distributed in Canada by Sterling Publishing,
c/o Canadian Manda Group, One Atlantic Ave., Suite 105
Toronto, Ontario, Canada M6K 3E7

Distributed in the U.K. by:
Guild of Master Craftsman Publications Ltd.
Castle Place 166 High Street, Lewes, East Sussex
England, BN7 1XU
Tel: (+ 44) 1273 477374
Fax: (+ 44) 1273 478606
Email: pubs@thegmcgroup.com
Web: www.gmcpublications.com

Distributed in Australia by Capricorn Link (Australia) Pty Ltd., P.O. Box 704, Windsor, NSW 2756
Australia

If you have questions or comments about this book, please contact:
Lark Books
67 Broadway
Asheville, NC 28801
(828) 236-9730

Printed in China

ISBN 1-57990-240-5 (hbk.) 1-57990-379-7 (pbk.)

CONTENTS

IN THE YEAR 2002 ONE OF THE WORLD'S
BEST-LOVED AND MOST HUGGABLE CULTURAL ICONS TURNS 100 YEARS OLD.
WELCOME TO THE PARTY!

Your specific reason for celebrating the teddy bear's 100th birthday may depend on where you reside in the vast universe of teddy fans. But whether you make them, collect them, remember one with great fondness, or have just recently realized how irresistible they are, you can't—according to lots of different experts—help but love them.

Since the first teddy appeared on store shelves in 1902, he and his confrere bears have been serving as confidants, confessors, comforters, and loyal sidekicks. They've been dragged around by one arm, slept with, cried on, and nuzzled until they're threadbare. They've also been written about, sung about, illustrated, animated, and used to market everything from breakfast cereal to hot water bottles. Each year, millions are sold around the world as gifts for bear lovers ranging from newborns to sweethearts. No one seems to know exactly why teddy bears have such an enduring hold on our imaginations and hearts, but the theories abound:

THE MYSTIC'S THEORY

Many early cultures revered real bears as embodiments of sacred healing and teaching. Their cycle of hibernating in the winter and awakening each spring offers us a model of spiritual renewal. Drawing on the power of their real-life counterparts, teddy bears convince us that everything will be better in the morning.

THE PSYCHOLOGIST'S THEORY

For a century, we've sewn into teddy bears the most desirable and innocent of human qualities, traits, and features. Teddy bears are perfect combinations of naiveté, spiritedness, earnestness, and good will. In short, they're fantasy versions of how we want everyone else to be.

THE ANTHROPOLOGIST'S THEORY

Humans have a fascination with bears for deep, unconscious reasons beyond our control. We identify with them because they can walk upright, their eyes are in the front of their faces, and they use mannerisms that make them seem almost human. In their teddy bear form, these wild animals we've watched from a distance since prehistoric times are transformed into accessible, cuddly friends.

THE BEHAVIORAL SCIENTIST'S THEORY

We now have research-supported proof that hugs (a teddy bear specialty) help lift spirits and calm anxieties.

THE AVERAGE BABY'S THEORY

Anna is 10 months old. She can't talk yet. She can't read. She doesn't understand theories, and she's never been coached on how to respond to cultural icons. But here's what Anna did when she and her father happened upon the photo shoot for this book. He asked what all the picture-taking was about. We held out a teddy bear to show them. Anna smiled, then squealed, then opened her arms wide for the bear. When we gave it to her, she immediately hugged it to her chest and cooed.

We may not be able to nail down the specific reason for teddy's appeal, but the phenomenon is undeniable. There's something about teddy bears that causes us to soften and open our arms and hearts wide. They give people of all ages permission to let down their guard. To let out a spontaneous "awwww." To unabashedly admit—no, *demonstrate*—that it's human instinct to hug a small, snuggly, friendly version of a bear and feel better for it.

We think 100 years of that is something to celebrate—enjoy the festivities!

HOW TO USE THIS BOOK

The first thing you should pay attention to when you set out to use this book is that it's a printed-and-bound celebration of teddy bears. That means you're not *required* do any more than sit back, flip through its pages, and enjoy the party; there's plenty to keep you entertained, from teddy bear traditions and trivia to photographic tours of teddy bears past and present.

If, on the other hand, your celebrating style is more active, you may want to make a teddy bear or two of your own. To meet your needs, we've included a thorough section on the basics of bearmaking, three master patterns with instructions, and—best of all—proof (thanks to a group of top artists who got in on the celebration early) that you can use those master patterns to make nearly any style of bear you can imagine.

THE THREE MASTER PATTERNS & INSTRUCTIONS

The first of the three master teddy bear patterns is super simple, just a single pattern piece with an optional extra piece for adding dimension to your bear's face. The second pattern is somewhat more involved (more pieces, which means more cutting, fitting together, and sewing). And the third pattern is for a traditional jointed bear, whose arms, legs, and head will move once you install the hardware that holds them together. The master pattern you choose and its accompanying instructions will serve as your primary guide for making your bear. The master patterns are at the back of the book, on pages 132 to 136. The master instructions precede each of the three teddy bear project sections.

HOW A GROUP OF DESIGNERS INTERPRETED THEM

We started the party a bit ahead of schedule on this end by inviting a group of teddy bear artists, dollmakers, sewers, and fiber artists to use the book's master patterns and instructions to come up with their own original teddy bears. The result, The Parade of Project Bears, begins on page 39. The whimsical bears this talented group came up with showcase an imaginative variety of materials, colors, and styles. A few are traditional-looking bears. Most are less conventional—celebrating just how versatile teddy bears can be. Together, they demonstrate the wonderful range of bears you can make from one of three basic patterns. Each project bear is accompanied by additional instructions for making that specific bear.

Once Upon a Time…the world was a cold, dark, scary place. It was full of strangers and sometimes even monsters. Not to mention long nights and thunderstorms and creepy places like unlit hallways. And little kids had to face it all alone.

It was 1901, and the teddy bear hadn't yet been invented.

Like any good story, the one about how the teddy bear came to be

changes a bit, depending on who's doing the telling. But all versions mark

1902 as the year a stuffed, jointed toy resembling a bear cub first appeared

on the market. And every teller agrees that the enchanting little creation

helped make the world a friendlier place for people of all ages.

The original Washington Post *cartoon by Clifford Berryman, depicting U.S. President Teddy Roosevelt sparing the life of a bear cub*

Courtesy of the Theodore Roosevelt Collection, Harvard College

LOADED FOR BEAR IN MISSISSIPPI

Part of the story starts with United States President Theodore Roosevelt and a trip he took to the backwoods of Mississippi to hunt bear. The party failed to spot a single target during its four days out, and, as the expedition drew to a close, members worried that it would seem unpresidential for Roosevelt to go home empty-handed. At the last minute—according to the most dramatic version of the tale—several other hunters managed to capture a small cub, tether him to a tree, and clear the way for the president to claim his prize. But Mr. Roosevelt refused to shoot such a frightened and pitiful target, and shooed the little bear back to its mother.

THE RESPONSE BACK HOME

Political cartoonist Clifford Berryman, who was traveling with the president's hunting party, was moved by Roosevelt's compassion and sportsmanship. He immortalized the incident in a cartoon, "Drawing the Line in Mississippi," which ran in the *Washington Post* on November 16, 1902, and touched the hearts of the American public (so much so that Berryman included the cartoon's appealing little bear character whenever he portrayed the President from then on).

The cartoon and its story did more than tug at the heartstrings of Morris Michtom, a recent immigrant from Russia who ran a small candy and novelty shop in Brooklyn, New York. It inspired a new product. He asked his wife, Rose, to stitch a jointed bear cub resembling the cartoon character. She did, and he promptly displayed it in his shop window along with a slogan that stuck: "Teddy's Bear."

MEANWHILE, IN GIENGEN, GERMANY

About the same time Rose Michtom was stitching her first bears in Brooklyn, Margarete Steiff, a successful German dressmaker, was endearing herself

to the children of the town of Giengen by giving them small stuffed elephants made from her shop's felt scraps. The toys were so successful that she added them to her apparel line. Then her nephew, Richard, came up with an idea for expanding her stuffed-toy offerings. After spending hours sketching bears at the Stuttgart Zoo, he created a toy bear made of mohair, with a head and limbs that moved. In 1902, the same year the stuffed-bear craze was beginning to sweep the United States, the Steiff Company introduced its first models of jointed bears.

A HAPPY CONVERGENCE OF BEARS

It doesn't seem to matter who technically got their bears to market first; the teddy bear fad took hold, and there were more than enough buyers to go around.

The Michtoms in Brooklyn couldn't make enough bears on their own to meet demand, so they founded the Ideal Novelty and Toy Company, which operated successfully (with teddy bears as the cornerstone product) until 1984. Legend has it that Morris Michtom wrote President Roosevelt

Workers assembling teddy bears at Germany's Hermann factory, circa 1950.

One of the original teddy bears Morris and Rose Michtom created through their Ideal Novelty and Toy Company. He now resides at the Smithsonian Institution in Washington, D.C.

early on, asking for permission to use his name to help market their cuddly creations. Roosevelt's response? He doubted his name would mean much to the stuffed-bear business, but they were welcome to use it. They never patented it, however, and "teddy bear" soon became the common name for the many stuffed-bear toys that began to appear.

The Steiffs took their bears to the Leipzig Toy Fair in 1903. They were nearly overlooked until the last day, when a toy buyer for the large New York department store George Borgfeldt and Co. spotted the Steiff bears and immediately ordered 3,000 of them. That purchase started what became known as the Barenjahre (Bear Years) in Germany, a period between 1903 and 1908 when the number of teddy bears produced annually grew from 12,000 to nearly one million, and German bears found their way to homes around the world. By 1905, the Steiff bears were legally protected by their now-famous "button in the ear" trademark.

One hundred years later, the teddy bear fad has become a firmly established tradition—and one that's stronger than ever. Today, mass production of bears continues to flourish, with countries including New Zealand, Japan, Australia, the Netherlands, Austria, Switzerland, and others getting into the game. In addition, a whole new international industry of handmade art bears— fueled in great part by adult collectors—has exploded in the last few decades.

Most important, for a century now, the world has seemed a little less scary, monsters haven't always been so fierce, and nighttime trips down the hall haven't been quite so long, dark, or lonely. No wonder the teddy bear seems destined to live happily ever after.

A U.S. teddy bear factory in operation, circa 1930

Courtesy of the V&A Picture Library

TEDDY BEAR DESIGN TIMELINE

A

visual tour

of how teddy styles

have changed

with

the times

EARLY 1900s

The very first teddy bears—and their predecessors, bear automatons and stuffed toys called bruins, which stood on all fours or rolled around on wheels—weren't cuddly, round caricatures. They looked very much like real, live bears, with long limbs, humped backs, and pointed muzzles. They were made with brown boot-button eyes and a newly invented material: mohair plush. Manufacturers loved mohair, because it was much less expensive than the real fur that had been used to make other stuffed animal toys. Their mouths and noses were hand-stitched with brown or black thread, their paw and foot pads were most often made of felt, and they were stuffed with wood wool (also known as excelsior), made of long, fine wood shavings chopped into shorter strands.

Above and right: The earliest teddy bear designs were developed by studying and sketching real bears.

Far right (top): This Steiff bear named "Henrietta" was made by the famous German company in 1910.

Far right (bottom): Early bears, like this one created by the Hermann company of Germany, were frequently mounted on wheels.

Right bottom: Teddy bears manufactured in 1909 (left) and 1908, by Germany's Gebrüder Bing company

Previous page: - Known as "The Cattley Toys," this collection of teddy bears and other animals, dating from about 1906, originally belonged to one family's five children.

Courtesy of The Bear Museum in Petersfield, Hampshire, United Kingdom

Courtesy of Eric Kluge of Gebr. BING Inc., founded in 1865 in Nuremberg, Germany

1920s

As buttoned boots became less fashionable (making the buttons less common), blown-glass teddy bear eyes took over. Also during this time, kapok stuffing, the same material that had been used to fill life jackets during World War I, was popularized by British teddy bear companies. They preferred it over wood wool for its lighter weight, cheaper cost, and more hygienic quality. Especially typical of teddy bears produced in the 1920s and '30s were cardboard-reinforced feet.

Courtesy of Eric Kluge of Gebr. BING Inc., founded in 1865 in Nuremberg, Germany

Courtesy of The Bear Museum in Petersfield, Hampshire, United Kingdom

Far left: Germany's Gebrüder Bing manufactured not only teddy bears, but toys of all kinds, plus products ranging from typewriters to carburetors. Here, a 1920 Bing bear is pictured with one of the company's early record players.

Left: "Mr. Fluffy" was manufactured by the British toy company Chad Valley in 1923. He features glass eyes, which began to replace boot-button eyes during this period, and was one of the earliest teddy bears made with kapok stuffing.

Bottom: A series of short-haired silk plush bears manufactured by Germany's Hermann company in the 1920s.

925/40   925/60 B   960/60 B   960/50
  Serie 925   B=lenkbarer Kopf   Serie 960

1930s

Below left: "Heinrich," made circa 1935, is an example of the German firm Schreyer and Company's popular Yes/No bear, which is highly collectible today. With the help of a wire running up his body, his tail can be used as a lever to make him nod or shake his head.

Below right: "Bingie," produced as a part of a family of novelty teddy bears by the Merrythought company throughout the 1930s, was designed to appeal to very young children. Made to resemble a bear cub, he features stocky arms, short legs that are unjointed, and extra-soft kapok stuffing. Notice the trademark tag on his foot; trademarks were included on most manufactured teddy bears by this time.

By the 1930s, most major teddy bear manufacturers had patented trademarks that they attached to their bears in the form of permanent buttons or embroidered labels. (Before this time, few manufacturers labeled their bears, making it tricky today for collectors to trace the provenance of some of the earliest bears.) Also during this period, a treated muslin called Rexine was developed and became a popular material for teddy bear paw and foot pads until about 1960. (After that time, it was no longer available. Today, artists making collectors' bears authentic to this period use tightly woven cotton fabric painted with quick-drying acrylic as a substitute.) Bears that required less labor and cost to produce began to appear during the Depression era. The cheaper bears typically lacked all extras: jointing systems were simplified or nonexistent, limbs were shorter, material was less expensive (cotton flannel, for example, instead of mohair plush), and claws were seldom embroidered.

Courtesy of the V&A Picture Library

Courtesy of The Bear Museum in Petersfield, Hampshire, United Kingdom

1940s

After World War II, teddy bears in general had larger, more rounded heads, flatter muzzles, straighter backs, and shorter limbs. Immediately following the War, rationing continued to create a shortage of materials, but soon, a whole new world of options opened up in the form of materials made from synthetic fibers. As acrylic, nylon, and artificial silk plush began to be produced on woven backing, they were used to make the first washable, nearly indestructible bears, along with bears in various colors. Real sheepskin—both dyed and natural—was also a popular bearmaking material in the '40s. After 1939, kapok was in short supply, so bears of this period were commonly stuffed with waste from cotton and woolen mills.

Below left: This homemade wartime bear from England was made from an old woven-wool coat.

Below right: Designed to comfort English children during World War II, this gas mask case comes with a friendly attachment, a 10-inch (25.4 cm) plush teddy bear in felt clothing.

Courtesy of The Bear Museum in Petersfield, Hampshire, United Kingdom

Courtesy of The Bear Museum in Petersfield, Hampshire, United Kingdom

1950s AND '60s

By this period, teddy bears were looking less and less bear-like. With large heads, stubby limbs, and soft, colorful, synthetic "fur," they had evolved, in great part, from realistic bear replicas into cuddly comfort providers. In the '50s, molded glass and plastic eyes were the type most commonly used; they're still what you're likely to find on manufactured bears today. The 1950s also ushered in black molded rubber noses and an array of new options for paw and foot pads, including velveteen, leather, suede, and synthetic materials such as suedette and leatherette. Finally, to the delight of moms everywhere, plastic-foam stuffing appeared on the scene, making machine-washable bears a reality.

Top left: The "Cheeky" bear design was registered by the Merrythought company in 1957 and produced in a variety of sizes and basic styles. It's an excellent example of the era's distinctly un-bear-like teddy bears. The line's name is said to have been inspired by a member of the British Royal Family who saw one of the bears at a trade show and said, "What a cheeky looking bear."

Top right: This bear, manufactured by Wendy Boston Playsafe Toys Ltd. in the 1950s, is an example of one of the first machine-washable teddies made entirely from synthetic materials. The Wendy Boston firm introduced the idea.

Bottom left: A series of mohair bears manufactured by Germany's Hermann company in the 1950s.

Bottom right: One of the bears in H.G. Stone & Co. Ltd.'s Hugmee line, "Leon" plays a lullaby when wound up. (Earlier Hugmee bears played music when their bodies were pressed.) "Leon" was manufactured in 1962, and features plastic safety eyes and a printed tag stating that he is safe for children after being "Awarded the Certificate of the Royal Institute of Public Health and Hygiene."

Courtesy of The Bear Museum in Petersfield, Hampshire, United Kingdom

Courtesy of the V&A Picture Library

Far left: Some modern art bears are painstakingly hand distressed to give them the worn and well-loved look of heirloom bears. This one was made by designer Bette Carter.

Left: With his rounded body, stumpy limbs, safety eyes, plastic nose, and golden flame-resistant fur, "Darren," made by Pedigree Soft Toys, Ltd. in 1975, is an excellent example of one of the earliest modern bears manufactured to be cuddly looking and completely safe for children.

MODERN BEARS

T he worldwide economic recession of the 1970s caused the teddy bear industry to slip into temporary hibernation. When teddies reemerged in full force, they had taken on two distinct forms.

One form is synthetic, cuddly, safe for children and all their wear and tear, and, when the day is done, fully washable. It's produced, for the most part, by multinational toy companies who play the biggest role today in the production of child-safe toy bears. The second form of the modern teddy bear is less a plaything and more a work of art. Growing numbers of teddy bear artists create these art bears for the burgeoning collectors' market. And in true teddy bear style, there's a story behind how this second form came to be.

In the late 1960s, British actor Peter Bull began championing the rights of teddy bears everywhere (and penned the first real survey of teddy bear history, *The Teddy Bear Book*). He encouraged adults to come clean about the fact that many still owned their childhood bears (or deeply regretted that they didn't). His celebrity brought his cause plenty of attention and helped set the stage for a generation of adult collectors. By about a decade later, thanks in great part to his efforts, a new art form had emerged—teddy bears designed and created not as toys, but as objects of art (not to mention adult affection). Some are based on traditional styles and are made using authentic methods and materials. Others build on the basic form in wildly creative ways. You'll see examples of both, submitted by teddy bear artists from around the world, in our Teddy Bear Gallery, beginning on page 102.

BEARMAKING BASICS

MATERIALS

No hidden surprises on the list of materials you need to make a teddy bear. Basically, you'll need some fabric and something to stuff it with—and if you're making a jointed bear, you'll need the hardware that holds it together.

FABRICS

When was the last time you had an excuse to ponder the subtle yet undeniably delightful distinctions among plush, furry, cuddly, and strokable? The fact that you get to choose a fabric may be all the reason you need for making a teddy bear.

■ MOHAIR ■

Mohair, a natural-fiber material made from angora goat fleece, is the teddy bear fabric for traditionalists. It's got the soft shiny qualities we've associated with stuffed animals since the crib, and it manages to be hard-wearing and luxurious at the same time. It also comes in a wonderful range of pile lengths, finishes, and colors (classic golds and browns to bright blue). Pile lengths typically run from ⅛ to 1 inch (3 mm to 2.5 cm). Finishes include everything from distressed, curled, dense, and sparse to tipped with a contrasting color (for a frosted appearance). Most mohair is manufactured in England and Germany, and sold primarily through teddy bear suppliers (who will often send

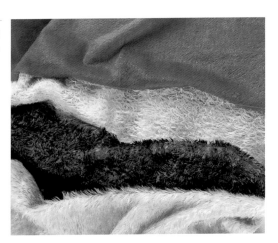

Assorted natural and dyed mohair fur

you samples to examine before you buy). Be sure to take a look at the woven backing as well as the fur itself. You want a backing that is flexible but not too soft; it's got to be workable but also hold its shape. And look for a backing that is closely woven, so it won't unravel during cutting and sewing. (By the way, when the fleece that makes the material comes from South American llamas rather than goats, it's called *alpaca*. Alpaca is quite similar to mohair and used in exactly the same way.)

■ SYNTHETIC FUR ■

Compared with mohair, synthetic fur is typically less expensive, easier to find in fabric shops, and available in a wider range of colors. Shop carefully, though. It varies a great deal in quality. Some synthetic furs have a woven backing, just like

mohair, which allows them to resist stretching and make a firm bear. Others have a knitted or jersey backing, which tends to stretch. If you use it, be especially careful not to overstuff your bear. With synthetic fur, it's also a good idea to carefully check the pile to make sure it's not prone to matting or shedding. Many mohair suppliers also sell high-quality synthetic fur.

■ OTHER FABRICS ■

As you'll see in the pages that follow, nontraditional teddy bears can be made from countless non-fur fabrics, from old quilts, coverlets, and blankets to upholstery fabric, coat fabric, wool tweed, and velveteen. Like synthetic fur, some of these other fabrics have lots of stretch to them, meaning you'll need to be careful not to overstuff your bear so it doesn't lose its shape. If you're using a fabric with a loose weave, stabilize it with a lightweight fusible backing before cutting out your pattern.

■ FABRICS FOR PAWS AND FOOT PADS ■

Suede, ultrasuede, wool felt, velveteen, and leather are all used for embellishing bear paws and feet with pads. Natural materials often make for more authentic-looking bears. Synthetic fabrics, such as ultrasuede, are typically harder wearing—which you may want if you anticipate that the bear you're making will be frequently pulled around by the paw.

Alpaca fur

Synthetic fur

Wool felt and Ultrasuede for paw and foot pads

STUFFING MATERIAL

A teddy bear that isn't huggable is hardly worth the bother. You've got several options for giving yours just the right bulk.

Polyester filling is the most popular and easiest to work with. It's clean, safe, and packs well to create a firm, evenly filled bear. High-loft varieties of polyester filling are more effective than cheaper grades, which tend to be thin and dense and can compact down into lumps.

Plastic pellets are also a popular filling often used in conjunction with polyester to give the bear's middle section a characteristic sag. Don't substitute bean bag filling for the plastic pellets (those extremely light polystyrene balls won't create the same effect). And don't use plastic pellets in a child's bear without first placing them in a securely closed fabric bag.

Wood wool, also called excelsior, was once a popular teddy bear stuffing. Because the finely shredded wood isn't washable and can have a high dust content, it's not widely used as stuffing today (outside of those making historic collectors' bears). Wood wool does come in handy for stuffing bear snout areas; it's easier to drive a needle through when embroidering the nose later.

Kapok, a vegetable fiber, is another traditional bear stuffing that is less commonly used today in standard-size bears. Its fine fibers often detach and float around—and they can be allergenic.

JOINTING SYSTEMS

Teddy bears can be plenty lovable (and simpler to make), without jointing systems. But add rotating joints to the arms, legs, and head, and your bear has the added ability to sit, wave, and pose in any number of positions.

Most people who make jointed bears use hardboard disks and washers, which you can combine with either cotter pin joints or nuts and bolts. You'll likely need to order the hardboard disks from a company that supplies fabric and notions

Plastic pellets and kapok stuffing

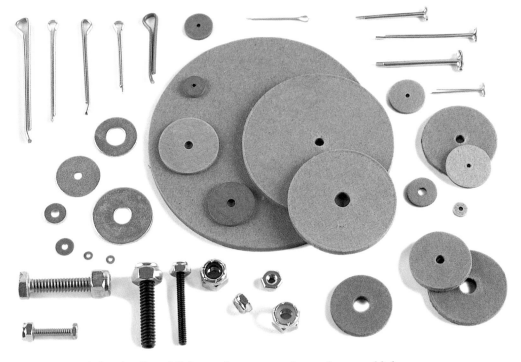

A plastic safety joint

Jointing supplies, including hardboard disks, washers, cotter pins, and nuts and bolts

for making bears. They come in various sizes and have a hole in the center. For one bear, you'll need 10 hardboard disks plus 10 metal washers. You can purchase the washers at your local hardware store, but they're less expensive if you get them from a bear supply company in bulk. Most bear suppliers will sell a set of disks and washers along with cotter pins or nuts and bolts for one bear.

Plastic joints, available at most craft stores, are not as stable as joints made with hardboard disks, but they'll work fine in most situations. Usually, there are three parts to a plastic joint: a disk shape with a plastic pin already in the center; a disk shape with a hole in the center; and a retaining washer.

Sewing thread and pearl cotton thread for embroidering facial features

TOOLS & SUPPLIES

Standard sewing supplies will cover most of what you need to make and assemble a teddy bear. The few tools you can't find at a sewing shop are readily available at craft or hardware stores.

SEWING NOTIONS

Though a sewing machine isn't essential for making the teddy bears in this book, one way or another, you'll be doing a lot of stitching. Here are the sewing notions you'll need.

Assorted hand-sewing and embroidery needles. You'll want to choose different sizes and types of needles for different tasks. For example, longer needles often work well for adding facial features when you're working through an opening in the back of your bear, darning needles are nice for embroidering noses, and some bearmakers prefer curved needles for closing openings or sewing on ears.

Dollmakers' needles (3½ inch [8.9 cm], 5 inch [12.7 cm], and 7 inch [17.8 cm]). These longer needles make it possible to pass thread through your bear's stuffed head when you're attaching the eyes.

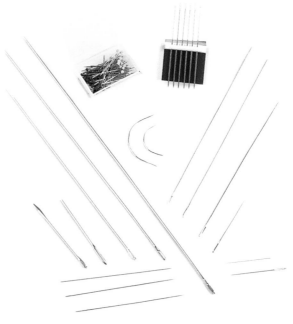

Assorted handsewing, embroidery, and dollmakers' needles

Polyester sewing thread to match your fabric. Sure, you can use cotton if you want a bear that's nothing but natural, but polyester thread is stronger.

Upholstery thread, carpet thread, or cordonnet to match your fabric. You'll use this sturdier thread for closing openings after stuffing your bear.

Assortment of pearl cotton thread. Choose from various colors and textures for embroidering facial features and claws. Numbers 3 and 5 are the most commonly used sizes. You can also use embroidery

Clockwise from upper left: nut drivers, stuffing sticks, awls, scissors, fabric markers, needle-nose pliers, locking-vise pliers, spring-action scissors, and forceps

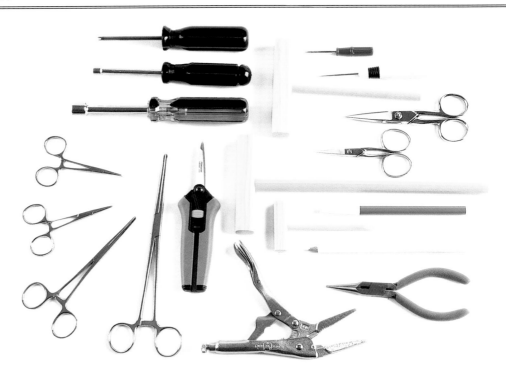

floss for your bear's features, though it may not create as smooth a look.

Color-headed pins. The colors will make the pins easier to identify in long-pile fabrics.

Sewing machine (optional). A straight-stitch machine will do. One with a zigzag stitch as well is ideal.

OTHER TOOLS

Fabric markers. Some sewers prefer chalk markers for tracing pattern pieces. Water-based markers come in handy for marking positioning guides for facial features.

Sharp-pointed scissors. Best for cutting out fabric.

Other scissors (optional). You may want standard craft scissors for cutting out pattern pieces and embroidery scissors for trimming threads. Both mustache-trimming scissors and hairdresser's thinning shears work well for clipping fur on areas where you're adding joints or for trimming your bear's muzzle.

Awl. For poking holes in your bear's fabric for eyes and joints.

Forceps. You'll use them to turn narrow pieces and stuff awkward corners.

Unsharpened pencil, wooden spoon, or stuffing stick. Professional sticks are available, but any blunt poking tool will help you pack the stuffing inside your bear.

Locking-vise pliers. Useful for holding joint "sandwiches" together while opening cotter pins or tightening bolts.

Needle-nose pliers. For opening and curling the ends

Pet brushes for teasing fur out of seams

of cotter pins and adding loops to eyes on wires.

Nut driver. Depending on your technique, you'll need one or two nut drivers for turning the nut and bolt on certain kinds of joints. They come in different sizes to match different bolts.

Pet brush. These tiny tools with wire bristles work perfectly for teasing fur out of seams after you've sewn your bear.

TECHNIQUES

Following are simple, step-by-step instructions that take you from marking your fabric pieces to embroidering your bear's facial features.

PREPARING YOUR PATTERN PIECES

Each of this book's patterns, beginning on page 132, must be enlarged on a photocopy machine according to the pattern notes. Turn your paper copies into sturdier templates by gluing the paper to thin cardboard or poster board and cutting them out once the glue is completely dry. If you'll be working with a fur fabric, make these sturdy templates for each piece the pattern instructions tell you to cut. For example, if the instructions accompanying an arm piece tell you to cut four pieces, two facing and two opposite, then you would prepare four pattern templates. If you'll be working with a thinner fabric that you can fold before cutting, you'll be able to cut out your facing pieces together, using only one pattern template.

MARKING & CUTTING OUT YOUR FABRIC PIECES

1. If you're working with fur fabric, determine which way the pile or nap of the fabric runs. You can do this easily by running your hand over the fibers. They'll lie down smoothly when you run it with the nap. Run your hand in any other direction, and the fibers will pull upward. On the back of your fabric, use an arrow to mark the direction of the nap (figure 1).

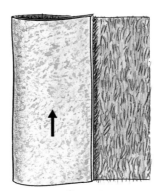

figure 1

2. Lay out your pattern templates for marking on the back side of your fabric, making sure the directional arrows on the templates match the one you marked to indicate the direction of the fabric's nap. If you're working with a fur fabric, lay out all of your pieces, including all of the facing (mirror

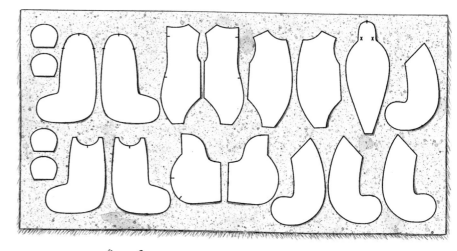

figure 2

image) and opposite pairs, on the back side of a single thickness of fabric (figure 2). If you're using a thinner fabric, you can fold the fabric, right sides together, and lay out just one template for each facing piece (since you'll be able to cut the two pieces at once). You'll still need to lay out two templates for each opposite piece (figure 3).

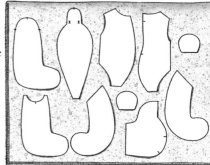

figure 3

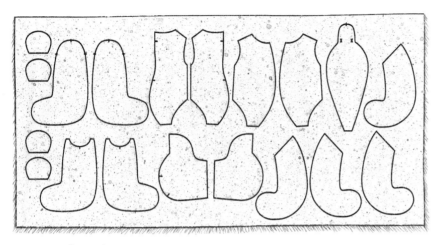

figure 4

3. Trace around the pattern templates with a fabric marker, and transfer all the markings (figure 4).

4. Lay your fabric on a clean, flat surface, and carefully cut out the pieces. If you're working with fur fabric, you want to snip more than cut, using scissors that are sharp to their points and snipping only the fabric backing, not the actual pile. This will be easier if you tilt your scissors up slightly, toward the backing, as you go.

Once you've cut out everything, it's a good idea to pair up all the pieces and arrange them in a rough bear position to make sure you've got all the pieces you need—and to give yourself a preview of how your bear will come together.

STITCHING THE PIECES TOGETHER

If you can sew a tight, straight seam—whether you're on friendly terms with a sewing machine or prefer to stitch by hand—you can make bears from any of this book's three basic patterns. The instructions for each tell you exactly which pieces to stitch together when. Meantime, here are some general tips.

• Pin or baste the pieces, right sides together (the sides with fur or the fabric's design), before stitching them. Color-headed pins are best for pinning, simply because they're easiest to see, especially if

you're working with fur. Position them so they're perpendicular to the edge of your fabric. If you're working with fur fabric, push the edges of the fibers inside as you pin or baste, so they won't get caught in the seam when you sew. (Once you turn the stitched pieces right side out, you can tease out those few fibers that do get caught.)

• With machine stitching, you can either sew two rows of straight stitches or sew one row of straight stitches, then add a zig-zag stitch in the allowance. (Zig-zagging the allowance is an especially good idea if you're using a fabric such as velveteen, which will ravel.)

• If you're sewing your bear by hand, you'll use these three basic stitches:

Backstitch. Double your thread and place small stitches close together. This is the primary stitch you'll use for sewing pieces together (figure 5).

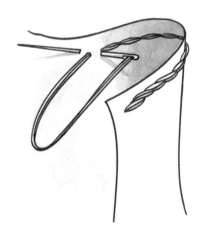

figure 5

Ladder Stitch. Anytime you want a hidden stitch, especially when you're closing openings after stuffing your bear, you'll use a ladder stitch (figure 6).

Whipstitch. If a hidden seam isn't necessary, such as when you're closing the bottom of your bear's ears, a whipstitch is quicker than a ladder stitch (figure 7).

figure 6

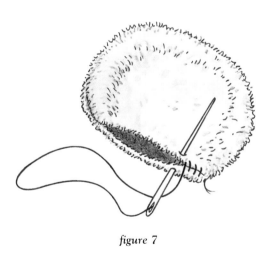

figure 7

TURNING YOUR BEAR

Some pieces of your bear can be turned right side out easily. Others, like the arms and legs, will take some gentle tugging with a pair of forceps.

1. Stick the forceps inside the piece, grab a section of the fabric at the other end (be sure you get a good grip on fabric and not just fur strands).

2. Lock the jaws and very carefully begin pulling the fabric out with the forceps.

3. When you get the end out, remove the forceps and finish turning the piece with your fingers.

4. Finally, you may need to use the locked forceps or a blunt stuffing stick to push out the seams from inside the piece.

TEDDY-MAKING TIP:

You may find it easier to turn sharply curved pieces (such as the muzzle, the top of the arms and legs, and the feet) if you carefully clip the seam allowance on these pieces first. Simply make straight cuts almost up to the stitching line along the curved areas.

ADDING JOINTS

If you're using the master pattern Teddy Bear #3 (page 134) to make a classic jointed bear, there are three basic systems for adding joints to the bear's arms, legs, and head. They all include pairs of disks. For each joint, you put one disk inside the arm, leg, or head, and the other inside the bear body. The difference in the systems is in how you connect the disks and hold them in place. Here, we've illustrated each system on small pieces of fabric.

■ TAP BOLT AND LOCKNUT JOINTS ■

This reliable system is, by far, the easiest system for beginners. The only drawback is that the materials are slightly more expensive than those for cotter pin joints. Washers and joints for use with tap bolts can have a ⅛-inch (3 mm) or a ¼-inch (6 mm) opening in the center, depending on the size of the bolt and nut. Tap bolts are just the regular hardware variety. Locknuts look like regular nuts, except that they have a small bit of plastic inserted into the center that keeps them from coming loose.

figure 8

figure 9

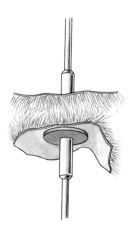

figure 10

1. With an awl, pierce holes in the joint markings, which you transferred earlier from the pattern to your fabric. Working on the inside of the limb or head you're attaching, place one metal washer followed by one hardboard disk onto the bolt, push the bolt through the hole in the limb or head, then push it into the body of the bear (figure 8).

2. On the end of the bolt inside the body, add another disk and washer. Secure the joint with a locknut (figure 9). You can easily hold the sandwich together with locking-vise pliers while you use a nut driver to tighten the locknut, or you can use a nut driver on either side of the joint, twisting them in opposite directions at the same time (figure 10). The locknut should be tightened so that the arm, leg, or neck move only slightly when the bear is unstuffed; they'll move more easily after the bear is stuffed. For a wobbly feel to the joints, don't make them quite as tight.

■ COTTER PIN JOINTS ■

Practice really does make perfect with this system. It also takes some hand strength, but many bearmakers will tell you it's worth it. Cotter pins make a lasting and secure joint, which is why they're used in most collectors' bears. The disks and washers you use with cotter pins typically have a ⅛-inch (3 mm) hole in the center.

1. With an awl, pierce a small hole in the joint markings, which you transferred earlier from the pattern to your fabric. Working on the inside of the limb or head you're attaching, insert a cotter pin in the center of one washer and one hardboard disk, push the pin through the hole in the limb or head, then insert the open end of the cotter pin into the body of the bear (figure 11).

2. On the inside of the body of the bear, insert the open end of the cotter pin into another disk and washer. Hold the assembled "sandwich" together (again, locking-vise pliers work well for this). Use

a pair of needle-nose pliers to open the cotter pin slightly. Curl each end of the cotter pin under so that it rests securely against the metal washer (figures 12 and 13).

■ PLASTIC JOINTS ■

Plastic joints are inexpensive, available in most craft stores, and safe for use in bears for children (their locking system is secure, so there's no danger of small parts falling off and making their way to little mouths). The disadvantage is that they're not as strong as other jointing systems.

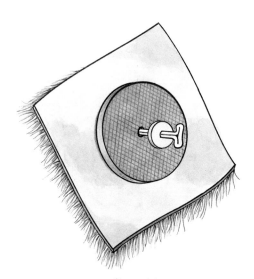

figure 11

figure 12

1. With an awl, pierce a small hole in the joint markings, which you transferred earlier from the pattern to your fabric. Working from the inside of the limb or head you're attaching, push the pin of the first disk through the marked hole and then into the body of the bear (figure 14).

2. On the inside of the body, push the disk with a hole onto the pin, then add the retaining washer (figure 15). You can tighten the hold by placing an old wooden spool over the pin, then tapping the spool lightly with a hammer.

It's especially difficult to tighten the head joint with this system. You'll need to determine if the pin is long enough to go though the neck and the body and still have length enough to connect securely with the second disk.

TEDDY-MAKING TIP:

Before you install your joints, apply fray retardant to the holes in the fabric where you'll be inserting them, and let it dry.

STUFFING YOUR BEAR

Here's where your bear takes shape—literally. How you mold its features as you fill it full of stuffing brings out its character. Whatever stuffing material you use (see Stuffings, page 20), work with small amounts as you begin poking it inside your bear, to avoid both unfilled gaps and lumps.

1. Start with the most difficult-to-fill areas, such as the nose, shoulders, and paws. Use a stuffing stick to make sure they're firmly and evenly stuffed and shaped the way you want before moving on.

2. Fill the perimeter areas of the bear next, and finally the middle. Places you may embroider, such as the face and paws, need to be especially firm. If

figure 13

figure 14

figure 15

HEY, THAT'S NOT A TOY!

Even though any standard thesaurus lists teddy bear as a synonym for toy, not all stuffed bears are considered safe enough to serve as playthings. If you're making bears to sell or give as gifts, it's important to know the difference between collectors' bears and child-safe bears.

COLLECTORS' BEARS

In the early days of bearmaking, all teddy bears were filled with natural stuffings and decorated with tiny button or glass eyes attached with twisted wire. Bears that were jointed were connected with metal pins and fiberboard disks. As a result, those early bears were flammable, and any features that came loose presented a risk to tiny hands and mouths. Lots of people still make teddy bears using traditional materials and techniques. Such bears are in demand as collectibles, but they're not considered safe for children.

CHILD-SAFE BEARS

Today, bears meant to be toys should be made with modern materials that make them safe for children of any age. Choose a manufactured stuffing such as polyester, plastic safety eyes, and a plastic safety nose if you're not embroidering the nose in place. For a jointed bear, use plastic safety joints, as well.

they're soft, scrunchy, or sagging, they'll be difficult to decorate.

3. When your bear is stuffed properly, you should be able to squeeze the closing seams together easily with your fingers. Once you're satisfied, use a ladder stitch to sew up all the closing seams but the one in the head and the back of the bear (you'll use those openings to add the bear's facial features).

ADDING FEATURES

If you've ever, at any time in your life, had a teddy bear, you know the rule. Your bear is the cutest, the sweetest, the best bear in the whole world. No one else, of course, can ever completely appreciate all that makes your bear so special. But how you fashion his facial features and other accents will give them a glimpse of his one-of-a-kind personality.

figure 16

■ THE NOSE ■

STEPS FOR A
TRADITIONAL EMBROIDERED NOSE

An oval is one of the easiest nose shapes for beginners to embroider. But if you think another shape would better suit your bear's personality, there are plenty of possibilities (see figure 16).

1. Before you start, play with placement and shape. Pick some designs from figure 16 that appeal to you, cut them out of felt, and experiment with them on your bear's snout.

2. Once you've decided which nose shape you want, you can either trace the felt piece with a water-based marker to create a placement guide or glue the actual felt piece in place and embroider over it.

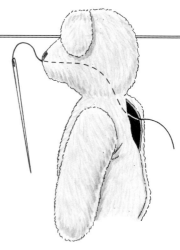

figure 17

3. You can embroider your nose with nearly any thread or yarn you like—both #3 and #5 pearl cotton threads work well—and choose a color that either complements or contrasts with your bear's face color. Work through the head seam or, with a non-jointed bear, through the opening in the back body seam, and use a long doll sculpture needle, which makes it more manageable to get from the opening to the nose area (figure 17). Begin at the top and center of the nose, and use a satin stitch (a long, flat stitch) to embroider from the center out to one side of the nose (see figure 18).

4. Return to the center top of the nose and embroider out to the other side. Make sure the strands of thread lie close together. Don't pull the stitching too tightly, but don't leave it so loose that gaps appear in the stitching. If you want more than one layer of thread on the nose, to build it up, repeat the process until you achieve the look you want. Switch to new thread if your strand becomes worn or gets too short to work with easily.

5. When you finish, pull the tail of the thread back through whichever opening you're using, and leave it until you finish the mouth.

figure 18

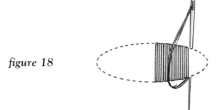

NOSE VARIATIONS

The artist airbrushed this colored rubber nose for added detailing.

The leather noses on these bears were hand-sewn on the snouts. The artist left openings for the nostril holes, stuffed the nose through the holes, then sewed the openings shut with upward stitches to emphasize the nostrils.

Noses embroidered with two colors of thread

An assortment of differently trimmed muzzles

TRIMMING THE MUZZLE

Regardless of the type of nose you choose, you'll want to consider trimming some or all of the muzzle area before adding it. Lightly trimming the nose area only will make it easier to attach your nose; shaving the muzzle more completely allows you to sculpt your bear's face to create different looks. Use sharp, pointed scissors and trim small amounts at a time, being careful not to clip the backing. Start at the top of the area you want to trim and work down. If you're removing fur from only the area where the nose will be, you can also use forceps to pluck pieces out.

SAFETY EYES & NOSES

*I*f you're making a bear for a small child and want to make sure the eyes and nose are securely fastened in place, you can opt for plastic safety features. Safety eyes and noses work in much the same way as plastic safety joints. They are held in place by either a lock washer or a plastic washer, which is pushed onto the stem that protrudes from the back of the eye or nose.

1. You need to have access to both sides of the bear's head to install safety features, so you'll add them before you stuff your bear. However, you may want to stuff the head temporarily when you begin, so you get a sense of its shape and know where you want to place the features.

2. Use an awl to make small holes where you want the eyes and nose (figure 19), then remove the stuffing.

3. One at a time, push the features into the head from the right side (figure 20).

4. On the stems inside the head, add the washers. Use a spool of thread over the stem to push the washers firmly in place, as far down as they'll go (figure 21)

figure 19

figure 20

figure 21

■ THE MOUTH ■

STEPS FOR A TRADITIONAL EMBROIDERED MOUTH

If you're already embroidering your bear's nose, it's easy to continue on and add a mouth.

1. Re-thread your needle, go in through the back or head opening, and come out at the bottom center of the nose.

2. From there, vary the length and angle of your stitches to create the expression you want. (Some of the most popular variations, ranging from enthusiastically cheerful to just plain content are illustrated in figure 22).

3. When you're finished, knot all the thread tails (including those from the nose), clip them, and push them into the stuffing. If you've been using the head opening, close it, using a ladder stitch and upholstery thread.

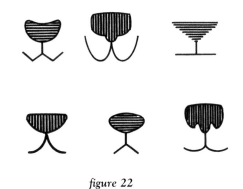

figure 22

BEST-LOVED BEARS IN THE WORLD

▪ MARTHE'S BEAR ▪

Name: Paddington ("of course")

Companion of Marthe Since: 1973

Origin: Though not an avid seamstress, Marthe's mother purchased a pattern and made Marthe her very own Paddington Bear. This delighted Marthe, a devoted fan of the Paddington books.

Favorite Activity: Like his fictional counterpart, this Paddington loves to hit the road. He accompanied Marthe throughout her childhood on adventures aboard airplanes, trains, ferry boats, subways, and taxi cabs around the world. Today, he lives a somewhat more settled life at her parents' home.

Special Skills: Partner gymnastics. For a time during her childhood, Marthe was addicted to cartwheels, which she frequently performed with Paddington in one hand.

A stitched-in open mouth painted with acrylic paint to add depth

This bear's mouth, open in song, was embroidered.

An open leather mouth featuring teeth and a tongue

These bears feature open mouths with embroidered teeth.

■ THE EYES ■

STEPS FOR ADDING TRADITIONAL BUTTON
OR GLASS EYES

Modern imitations of the shoe buttons once used almost exclusively for teddy bear eyes are available today. So are many variations of glass eyes, which became popular later. Some come with a loop on the back for attaching them. Others are sold by the pair on a long wire you've got to cut and loop yourself.

Preparing Eyes on Wires

1. Cut the wire in half with wire cutters (figure 23).

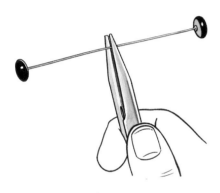

figure 23

2. Bend the wire over to form a U shape (figure 24).

3. Hold the wire with a pair of needle-nose pliers, and use your other hand to twist it around on itself (figure 25).

4. Once the wire is coiled, tuck the sharp end sticking out behind the loop (figure 26).

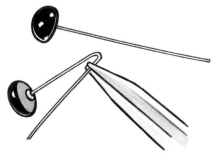

figure 24

figure 25

figure 26

Attaching Eyes

1. Begin by marking the eye positions with a water-based marker. Once you're sure of the positions, use an awl to make holes in the spots you marked. You may also want to trim a bit of fur from the areas where the eyes will go.

2. Thread a long needle with carpet thread, cordonnet thread, or dental floss, knot it into a double strand, and tie it onto the wire loop of one eye (figure 27). Crimp the wire loop with your pliers to further secure the thread.

figure 27

BEAR FACTS

AT THE RENOWNED STEIFF TEDDY BEAR FACTORY IN GERMANY, RUMOR HAS IT THAT THE WORKERS STUFFED TEDDY BEARS WITH RAGS AT THE END OF THE DAY IF THEY RAN OUT OF TRADITIONAL WOOD WOOL STUFFING.

figure 28

3. Push the needle into one of the eyeholes, and angle it down to come out through the back opening in the bear (figure 28) or, if you're working on a jointed bear, in the neck joint area.

4. Pull the eye securely into the hole. For extra security, you can add a dab of glue to the back of the eye. Knot off the thread in the bear's neck area, then repeat the process for the other eye.

5. When you're finished, if you've been working on a non-jointed bear, close the back opening with upholstery thread, using a ladder stitch.

EYE VARIATIONS

Beads glued to buttons form these eyes.

Eyes of faceted beads

Embroidered eyes

■ ADDITIONAL ACCENTS ■

EAR PLACEMENT AND EMBELLISHMENT

Teddy bear ears typically straddle the head's gusset seams, sit just below the seams on each side, or fall somewhere in between. How you position them exactly will help determine whether your bear is perky, pouty, or an especially good listener. You can also play with contrasting fabrics for the ears, or even darken the inside of the ears with paint (see page 36) to give them a more realistic look.

EYELASHES

Maybe unadorned button eyes don't give your bear quite the flirtatious flair you know she deserves. Here are two easy ways to make a bear's eyes flutter.

Eyelashes: Version 1

(This version is used on the Autumn Ted project, page 61.)

1. Using two strands of thread, make long loop stitches in a curve above your bear's eyes.

2. Clip the loops to create individual lashes.

Eyelashes: Version 2

1. Cut two pieces of long-pile fur, each about ¼ inch (6 mm) larger than your bear's eyes.

2. Make a hole in the center of each piece of fur with an awl, then push the shaft of an eye through each hole.

3. Install the eye as usual, with the lash pieces attached.

4. Trim and shape the lashes to suit your bear's style.

EYEBROWS

Most teddy bears are pros at showing concern. Others are perpetually surprised. And a few have even been known to be grumpy. The cock of an

EAR VARIATIONS

eyebrow can tell you all you need to know about your bear's basic demeanor. If you're already embroidering a mouth and nose, it's a simple matter to move up a few inches and add some stitches that frame the eyes. Figure 29 shows some easy-to-create options.

figure 29

PAWS

Whether you want realistic-looking paw pads or jewel-toned (and appropriately friendly) claws, there are ways to decorate your bear's feet, hands, fingers, and toes that range from traditional to fanciful.

Paw Pads

1. Cut shapes for the pads out of glove leather, suede, felt, or any other material you choose. (Cut the shapes a little larger than you want the finished pads to be, so you can turn their edges under slightly when you sew them in place.)

2. Either trim the fur from the entire paw, or lay the pads on the paw to determine their position, then trim away fur from those spots only.

3. Sew the pads in place with a ladder stitch, turning their edges under as you go. If you like, leave a

small opening on each, use forceps to stuff each pad with a small amount of soft polyester stuffing, then finish stitching the pad in place (figure 30).

Embroidered Claws

1. On the edge of the paw, place a color-headed pin for each claw you want to stitch.

2. Using a long embroidery needle and embroidery thread, secure a stitch on the fur side of the paw, then come through on the other side, about 1 inch (2.5 cm) below the first pin.

3. Loop the thread up, and come back in on the fur side, just beyond the first pin. Next, come out about 1 inch (2.5 cm) below the second pin. Continue this process until you've embroidered all the claws. Finish with a backstitch on the fur side of the paw, then bring the thread out on one side of the paw (figure 31).

ACCENT COLOR

If you want your teddy bear's face to feature some of the natural shading a real bear's does, simply brush on a little acrylic fabric paint. The insides of the ears, the areas above the eyes, and the part of the muzzle below the nose are the places where a darker color will add interesting dimension. Brush the paint on in thin layers with a medium-size brush. Once it's completely dry, smooth out the painted areas with a stiff wire brush.

BEAR FACTS

ACCORDING TO TEDDY BEAR LORE, ONE OF THE REASONS TEDDY BEARS SHOW UP ON THE WALLS OF PLACES SUCH AS NURSERIES AND DENTIST'S AND PEDIATRICIAN'S OFFICES IS THAT THEY HAVE A CALMING EFFECT ON CHILDREN.

HUMAN FASCINATION WITH BEARS GOES BACK TO THE TIME OF THE NEANDERTHALS, WHO USED CAVE BEAR SKULLS IN RITUAL SACRIFICES.

figure 30

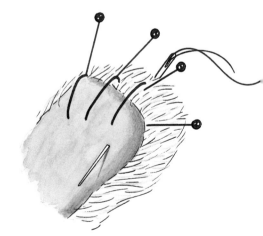

figure 31

STYLIZED PAWS

Suede paw pads with needle-sculpted claws

Appliquéd paw pads

Handmade resin claws

Paw pads painted with acrylic paint

PARADE OF PROJECT BEARS

This chapter is full of teddy bears you can make, with the projects divided into three sections. Each section begins with master instructions for making a basic teddy bear from its corresponding master pattern (master patterns appear on pages 132 to 136). Following the master instructions is a variety of project bears created by our teddy bear designers. Each project comes with its own special instructions for bringing that bear to life.

·39·

MASTER INSTRUCTIONS

TEDDY BEAR #1: SINGLE PATTERN PIECE BEAR

Pattern: page 132

MATERIALS & TOOLS

Fabric marker

Fabric approximately twice the size of the pattern (For a 14-inch [35.6 cm] bear, you'll need about ½ yard [.45 m] of 36 to 45-inch [91 to 114 cm] fabric, depending on how the pattern or nap runs.)

Sharp scissors

Color-headed pins

Polyester sewing thread to match fabric

Stuffing

Stuffing stick

1 pair of eyes

#3 or #5 pearl cotton thread for embroidering facial features (optional on some bears)

Upholstery thread, carpet thread, or cordonnet to match fabric

Sewing machine or thread and needles

INSTRUCTIONS

1.

Prepare the pattern pieces.

2.

Place the pieces on your fabric, mark them, and cut out two of the body pattern pieces. If you're not working with synthetic or thick fabric, you can fold your fabric in half, right sides together, and cut out

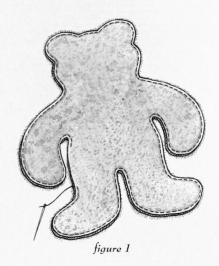

figure 1

both pieces at once. If you're using the optional face insert, cut one insert piece from an unfolded fabric scrap.

3.

Mark the openings on the sides of the pieces.

4.

If you're using the optional face insert, cut out the marked circular shape on the face of one body piece.

5.

Sew the two pattern pieces together, using a ⅜-inch (9.5 mm) seam allowance (which is built into the pattern), and leaving the opening between the markings on the side (figure 1). If you're hand-sewing,

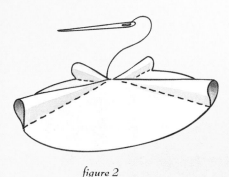

figure 2

use polyester all-purpose thread, doubled, and backstitch the seam. Or, you can sew it twice with small stitches. If you're using a machine, either sew two rows of straight stitches or sew one row of straight stitches and zigzag the allowance outside the first row of straight stitches. This is especially necessary if you're using a fabric like velveteen that will ravel.

6.

Carefully clip the seam allowance along the pattern's sharply curved lines (to make turning easier), and turn the bear right side out.

7.

If you're using the face insert, sew the darts on that piece (figure 2). Pin the insert into place for a muzzle, and either hand or machine sew it into place (figure 3).

8.

If you're using plastic safety features (eyes and/or a nose), insert them at this point, before stuffing your bear. Work through the side opening.

9.

Use polyester filling (or another filling of your choice) to stuff your bear. If you want a more realistic or floppy bear, stuff each arm and each leg, and then sew a row of hand or machine stitching at the shoulders and hips to form hinge joints. Stuff the body and finally the head. (You can also add hinge joints, machine or hand-sewn, to the neck and ears.) Bears intended for pillows do not really need the hinge joints.

10.

If you're using glass or button eyes or embroidering the nose or other features, add them, working through the side opening.

11.

Hand-sew the side opening closed with a ladder stitch and upholstery thread, carpet thread, or cordonnet, then knot off. Clip the threads close to the seam.

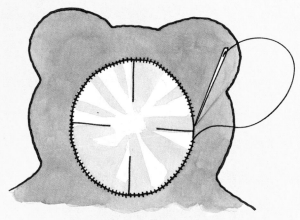

figure 3

Fuzzy Wuzzy Snuggly Bear

F uzzy Wuzzy Snuggly Bear's only real regret in life is that he seldom gets to have a complete conversation with anyone. People start off with good intentions. They look straight at him, pay him full attention. And then, pretty soon, their eyes start to get heavy. He begins noticing a familiar pattern of yawn after uncontrollable yawn. Pretty soon—it never fails— whoever it is he's been having a stimulating exchange with trails off in mid-sentence, begins nuzzling his fur, and, finally, curls up for a long and peaceful snooze. It's not that he minds being the fuzziest, snuggliest, most irresistible nap-time bear ever. But it does get unbearably quiet at times.

DESIGNER:
BETH HILL

WHAT YOU NEED

Teddy Bear #1 Master Pattern, page 132

Teddy Bear #1 Master Instructions, page 40

Teddy Bear #1 Materials & Tools, page 40

ADDITIONS & ADAPTIONS TO MATERIALS & TOOLS

• Body fabric: use 1/2 yard (.45 m) acrylic fur

• Ultra-leather nose

• Ribbon

INSTRUCTIONS

Follow the Teddy Bear #1 Master Instructions, adding the optional face insert and sewing the hinge joints. Finish your bear by adding a ribbon around his neck.

BEAR FACTS

OFTEN ENOUGH FOR THE FACT TO HAVE MADE ITS WAY INTO ARTICLES IN THE TEDDY BEAR TRADES, HOTEL CLEANING PEOPLE REPORT SPOTTING TEDDY BEARS IN ROOMS OCCUPIED BY BUSINESS TRAVELERS.

MERRY PRANKSTER HARLEQUIN BEAR

Don't let the serious look he mugged for the camera fool you. This theatrical little bear, with his kicky boots, jaunty hat, glittery fabric paint, and tinkling bells, has a penchant for play—not to mention mischief. Throughout the making of this book, his shenanigans surprised us, entertained us, and regularly tried our patience. (*Tell the readers he belongs in a home full of lots of active young boys who will give him a dose of his own medicine,* urged one bear who was a regular focus of our Merry Prankster's practical jokes.) Eventually, though, antics and all, his lively spirit won our hearts.

DESIGNER:
MARY STANLEY CASADONTE

INSTRUCTIONS

1.

Using both the Master Pattern and the Merry Prankster Harlequin Bear Patterns, page 138, cut out your fabric pieces as described in the Teddy Bear #1 Master Instructions. Be sure to cut the paw pads out of the velveteen.

2.

With the lightest color of fabric paint and the larger foam brush, coat the right sides of the bear body pieces, two facing sides of the shoes, and one triangle point on each hat piece.

3.

Use the ruler and pencil to lightly sketch a diamond-pattern grid on the bear body pieces. Cover one body piece entirely with the pattern. On the other (the one that will become the front of the bear), leave the head area plain.

4.

Use the two remaining paint colors and the smaller foam brushes to paint the diamond shapes. Paint the two remaining shoe pieces and the unpainted parts of the hat, as well.

5.

With the artist's brush, paint over all of your grid lines with gold paint. Let all of the pieces dry.

6.

Turn the edge of each paw pad under ¼ inch (6 mm), and sew each. On the right side of the body piece that will become the front of the bear, sew a pad in place on each paw.

7.

Sew the bear (adding the optional face insert, if you like) and stuff it, following the Teddy Bear #1 Master Instructions. (On the bear shown, the designer cut her face insert slightly smaller than the pattern piece and stuffed it firmly, to create a more prominently protruding snout.)

8.

Use the black and brown fabric paints to add facial features.

9.

With the right sides together, sew the shoes and the hat.

10.

Turn the shoes and hat right side out, turn the open seams on each ¼ inch (6 mm) under, and stitch them.

11.

Sew bells onto the points of the hat and shoes.

12.

Slip the hat and shoes onto your Merry Prankster Harlequin Bear and watch out! (Because this bear tends to be active, you may want to stitch his hat in place once you've positioned it where you want it.)

WHAT YOU NEED

Teddy Bear #1 Master Pattern, page 132

Merry Prankster Harlequin Bear Patterns, page 138

Teddy Bear #1 Master Instructions, page 40

Teddy Bear #1 Materials & Tools, page 48

ADDITIONS & ADAPTATIONS TO MATERIALS & TOOLS

- Body fabric: use ¾ yard (.7 m) porous, unbleached, medium-weight muslin

- ¼ yard (.25 m) of velveteen that complements your paint colors for paw pads

- Acrylic fabric paints in three complementary colors, plus gold, black, and brown

- 1 foam brush (2 inches [5.1 cm])

- 2 foam brushes (1 inch [2.5 cm])

- 1 artist's brush (¼ inch [6 mm])

- Ruler

- Pencil

- Fabric pens

- 5 ½-inch (1.3 cm) bells

BEARS ON THE BIG SCREEN

He's served as an indispensable prop. He's costarred with everyone from Tallulah Bankhead and Marlene Dietrich to Courtney Love and Santa Claus. And he's appeared as the headliner of his own shows. If anybody ever had a face the camera loves, it's the world's favorite stuffed celebrity, the teddy bear.

TOP TEN TEDDY FLICKS

THE NIGHT BEFORE CHRISTMAS, 1905

In this teddy bear motion picture debut produced by the Edison studio, a teddy bear is placed on a fireplace mantel by none other than Santa himself.

THE TEDDY BEARS, 1907

The members of the teddy bear troupe performing acrobatic feats in this stop-action animation movie are actually human performers in costume.

Mary Pickford and her only friend, her teddy bear, in *The Poor Little Rich Girl*

THE POOR LITTLE RICH GIRL, 1917

In this tear-jerker with a happy ending, "America's Sweetheart," Mary Pickford, plays a Manhattan child whose social-climbing parents have no time for her and whose governess is cruel. Fortunately, she has a teddy bear in whom she confides all.

Human acrobats in teddy suits in the 1907 film, The Teddy Bears

A doll-like creature herself, Shirley Temple was frequently photographed by her studios' publicity departments with dolls and—as shown here— teddy bears.

NURSE MARJORIE, *1920*

Mary Miles Minter stars in this romantic comedy set in a hospital. In a pivotal scene, she presents one of her favorite patients, a little boy who's lame, with an oversized teddy bear.

BLONDE VENUS, *1932*

A little boy's teddy bear is bedtime companion, good-luck token, and survivor of numerous family disasters in this Marlene Dietrich classic about a once-happy family stricken with trauma.

NOW AND FOREVER, *1934*

Shirley Temple was cast in one of her earliest films as the unwitting (who would ever suspect her?) courier of a teddy bear filled with stolen jewels.

JACQUELINE, *1956*

A faithful teddy bear helps a young Irish girl get her down-and-out father back on track in this delightful British movie.

DIE, DIE, MY DARLING! *1965*

It's not exactly light and happy fare, but a teddy bear does play a central role. Stage star Tallulah Bankhead stars in one of her few films as a deranged and jealous mother who blames her daughter-in-law for her son's death—and seeks comfort from his childhood teddy bear.

Mary Miles Minter in *Nurse Marjorie*, preparing to give a young patient a dose of love

The Museum of Modern Art/Film Stills Archive

BRIDESHEAD REVISITED, *1982*

It was a television miniseries, not a big-screen movie, but Brideshead Revisited still gave a teddy bear named Aloysius lots of play. He's the inseparable companion of a British aristocrat heading to Oxford in the 1920s.

THE PEOPLE VS. LARRY FLYNT, *1996*

Yes, we said The People vs. Larry Flynt, of all titles. In this controversial film, Flynt's wife, played by Courtney Love, clings to her teddy bear as a relic of her ruined childhood.

CONFETTI TEDDY

D espite the celebratory name—in honor, of course, of the multicolored streamers he sports on his chest—Confetti Teddy is an appealingly reserved reveler. You'll seldom see him swinging from a chandelier or taking a swim in a champagne fountain. (All his satin and soft-cotton pastel prevent him from that sort of carousing.) You'll find he's much more at home whispering comforting words of welcome from his favorite perch—on the edge of a bassinet.

DESIGNER:
YVONNE WILLIAMS

INSTRUCTIONS

WEAVING THE FRONT TORSO PIECE

1.

Put double-stick tape around all four sides of the loom.

2.

Fill the loom with strips of white ribbon running lengthwise (creating what is known in weaving as the warp). Place the ribbon strips closely together, leaving only a tiny space (about the size of a pin head) between each. Fasten the ends against the tape, and then cut off any extra ribbon. Once all the ribbons are in place, secure them with cellophane tape around the edges of the loom.

3.

With another strip of white ribbon, make a single knotted loop through the eye of your shuttle, and, beginning at one end, weave it over and under the warp ribbons (see figure 1). Cut the ends and secure them against the tape. Alternate white

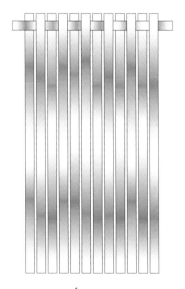

figure 1

WHAT YOU NEED

Teddy Bear #1 Master Pattern, page 132

Teddy Bear #1 Master Instructions, page 40

Teddy Bear #1 Materials & Tools, page 40

ADDITIONS & ADAPTATIONS TO MATERIALS & TOOLS

• ¼-inch-wide (6 mm) satin ribbon in spools of the following colors: white (2), green (1), blue (1), pink (1), yellow (1), lavender (1)

• ⅓ yard (.3 m) lightweight fusible interfacing

• Loom (Anything that is sturdy and has an opening large enough to weave a piece of fabric measuring about 8 x 8 inches [20.3 x 20.3 cm] for the torso. A picture frame works especially well.)

• Shuttle (You can find a drawstring threader in the notions department of most sewing stores.)

• Double-stick tape

• Cellophane tape

• Large piece of tissue paper

• Body fabric: use ½ yard (.45 m) white bridal satin (back and face piece); ½ to ⅔ yard (.45 to .6 m) white batiste (interlining); and small scraps of blue batiste (head), pink batiste (arms), and green batiste (legs)

• 15 mm eyes (2)

• A scrap of black felt for the nose

• Ribbon to make bow tie

• Craft glue

• Iron

---

and different colored ribbons as you continue to weave. Every few rows, straighten the ribbon and snug it against the row above.

4.

When you're finished weaving, cut a piece of fusible interfacing to cover the entire back of the woven piece, including the raw ends of the ribbon. Use an iron to fuse the pieces together, according to manufacturer's directions. Remove the fused piece from the loom, being careful not to pull the ribbons out of alignment when you remove the tape.

5.

Stitch around the edges of the square piece.

MAKING THE BEAR

1.

Prepare the body pattern and the face insert pattern, as described in the Master Instructions.

2.

Create additional pattern pieces for Confetti Teddy's multicolored front side by tracing the body piece onto tissue paper, marking lines to segment off the head, arms, and legs, then cutting those pieces away. Add a ⅜-inch (9.5 mm) seam allowance to the cut edges of the torso and to the cut edges of the head and limb pieces (see figure 2). (This process will create some excess seam allowance on the torso, which you'll trim later in step 11.)

3.

Working on the back of the white satin, use a fabric marker to trace one bear body and one face insert (including the dart marks). Apply fray retardant to the cut lines. When the retardant is dry, cut the pieces out.

4.

Out of white batiste, cut one complete bear body (using the Master Pattern) plus one head, two arms, and two legs (using the tissue-paper guides you created in step 2). You'll use these batiste pieces as interlining.

5.

Again using the tissue-paper guides, mark and cut one head out of blue batiste, two legs out of green batiste, and two arms out of pink batiste. On both the white and blue head pieces, cut out the small circle, over which you'll later sew the face insert.

6.

Baste the white batiste interlining pieces

to their satin or colored batiste counterparts, wrong sides together.

7.

Trace the shape of the torso on the back of the woven piece. Mark the location of the head, arms, and legs. Stay stitch inside the seam allowance to prevent the ribbon from coming apart, then cut out the torso.

8.

Stitch the darts on the face insert and sew around the insert, ⅜ inch (9.5 mm) in from the edge. Make V-shaped clips around the edge, turn it under, and finger press it.

9.

Center the face insert on the blue head piece (over the smaller opening you cut in step 5), secure it with pins, and stitch it in place.

10.

Pin or baste the colored head, arms, and legs to the woven torso, then stitch them in place and press the seams gently.

11.

Follow the Master Instructions for attaching the front and back body pieces, trimming any odd excess from the woven torso, if necessary, but making sure you leave the seam allowance intact at the side opening, where you will turn and stuff the bear.

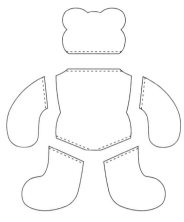

figure 2

12.

Follow the Master Instructions for turning, stuffing, and closing the bear. If you want to use safety eyes or embroider your facial features, add these elements before closing the bear. Otherwise, proceed according to the following steps.

13.

Cut a nose shape out of black felt and use a piece of pearl cotton thread or embroidery floss for the mouth. Glue the features in place (gluing is easier on the satin than stitching).

14.

Stitch the eyes in place.

15.

Tack a bow tie made of ribbon around your Confetti Teddy's neck.

TEDDY-MAKING TIP:

Use tape to gently position (and, if necessary, reposition) your Confetti Teddy's facial features before gluing them in place.

Bubbly Blue Bauble Bear

Like any self-respecting teddy bear, Bubbly Blue Bauble Bear tells an enchanting story about how he came to be. First, he explains, his designer was visited by her muse (*it's a tiny humming-bird fairy who flits around in her head and whispers creative ideas in her ears*). The muse planted visions of a miniature bear and reminded her how much she likes wearable art. Not long after, the design-er (who happens to love water) came upon a passage in the book she was reading that described a heavenly bath-room, complete with golden taps with jeweled handles that gushed perfumey, foamy, colored bubbles. The designer threaded a needle, stitched the two experiences together, and thus was born this tiny, bubble-bead encrusted, wear-able bear—a talisman and jewelry pin in one.

DESIGNER:
VICTORYA BLUE
LIGHTNING SNAKE

WHAT YOU NEED

Teddy Bear #1 Master Pattern, page 132

Teddy Bear #1 Master Instructions, page 40

Teddy Bear #1 Materials & Tools, page 40

ADDITIONS & ADAPTATIONS TO MATERIALS & TOOLS

• Freezer paper

• Body fabric: use a piece of cotton cloth to match your darkest bead (4 x 10 inches [10.2 x 25.4 cm]); a piece of fusible interfacing (4 x 10 inches [10.2 x 25.4 cm]); and a square of upholstery velvet for the face insert (1¼ inches [3.2 cm])

• Size 11 seed beads in mixed colors of your choice (You'll need several handfuls of beads for this project.)

• Several size 12 sewing sharps (You'll be maneuvering tight angles while sewing your beads in place, meaning your needle may break. No big deal if you have extras on hand.)

• Size A silamide waxed bead thread in a color that blends with your beads

• Two 3 mm black glass eyes for miniature bears

• One 6 mm black glass nose for miniature bears

• One 1-inch (2.5 cm) pin back

• Iron

INSTRUCTIONS

1.
Reduce the body pattern until it measures 3¾ inches (9.5 cm) high by 2⅞ inches (7.3 cm) wide. Reduce the face insert to a ⅞-inch (2.2 cm) circle.

2.
Trace the reduced patterns onto the unwaxed side of a piece of freezer paper, and cut them out to use as templates.

3.
Following the manufacturer's instructions, iron the fusible interfacing to the wrong side of the cotton cloth.

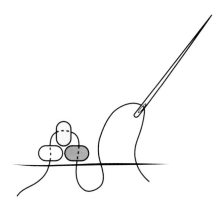

figure 1

4.

Fold the cloth in half, right sides together, and iron the freezer-paper body template to the interfacing. Do not cut out the body yet.

5.

Iron the freezer-paper face-insert template to the wrong side of the velvet, and cut the piece out.

6.

Using a very short stitch length, sew around the body template to stitch the two body pieces together. Be sure to leave the side opening for turning and stuffing. Begin and end with a back stitch.

7.

Carefully cut out the bear, leaving a ⅛-inch (3 mm) seam allowance. Leave a slightly larger allowance at the opening; the extra allowance will make it easier to close the opening after you've stuffed your bear.

8.

Remove the template and iron the body piece (pressing it flat) to set the stitches.

9.

Clip tiny slits in the seam allowance at the neck, under the arms, and between the legs, being careful not to cut through the stitching. If you like, add a bit of fray retardant to the points where you made the cuts.

10.

Use forceps (and some patience) to carefully turn the bear right side out.

11.

Stuff the bear as firmly as possible, so you have a good base for adding the beads. Sew the side opening shut.

12.

Mark the darts on the face insert, remove the template, and hand-sew the four darts.

13.

Position the insert on the bear's head, and use a ladder stitch to attach it. Sew three-quarters of the way around, stuff a small amount of stuffing under the insert to give it some dimension, then finish sewing.

14.

Sew the glass eyes and nose securely in place. You'll probably need to use an awl to make holes for the wires on the eyes and nose to pass through. After attaching these features, knot off at the back of the bear's head. (Your knots will be covered by beads when you finish the bear.) Embroider a mouth.

15.

Position and sew the pin back firmly to the "backbone" of the bear.

BEADING

The appliqué stitch you'll use for this bear is called a bouclé stitch. It creates a textural carpet of beads.

1.

Pull off about 1 yard (.9 m) of bead thread and tie a knot at one end of the thread. If you have trouble threading the needle, wet the eye of the needle, not the thread. The moisture will draw the thread to it.

2.

Anchor the thread on the body near the face insert. Take a stitch and pull tightly, to make sure it'll hold.

3.

String three beads (mixed colors), and pull them down onto the surface of the fabric. Take a small "tuck" stitch in the fabric, about two bead widths apart. Come back out as close to the beads as possible (see figure 1). The tuck stitch should be small enough so that the first and third bead touch and the second bead stands on end. Pulling the thread tightly is essential in getting the beads to lay correctly. Continue this process to bead the entire bear, covering the area around the face insert first, then beading the rest of the bear in sections. Choose bead colors and placement randomly; changing the direction and angle of the stitches creates the textural carpet effect. Crowding the beads together and pushing them into place with your fingernail helps prevent the fabric underneath from showing. When you come to the end of the thread, take several small stitches, knotting off as you go, then hide your thread in the bear. Place a drop of fray retardant on the knotted stitches, let it dry, and then bead over the stitches.

TEDDY BEAR TLC

❧

If teddy bears could talk, they'd tell you that serving as the recipient of a lot of love is hard work. You get slept on, cried on, spilled on, tugged on, dragged around by one limb, and frequently squashed. Years later, when your once-constant companion still wants you around but not on display every day, you endure dusty attics, damp garages, cramped storage boxes, and fabric-eating insects.

After all that, most bears could use a little reviving. Others, after maybe a losing encounter with an overly affectionate puppy or the tragedy of a house fire or flood, may need expert emergency care. Both categories of bears are treated by skilled hands and warm hearts at teddy trauma centers, emergency rooms, hospitals, and even wellness clinics around the world. These cleverly titled repair businesses are run by teddy bear restoration artists who are adept at everything from touching up family heirlooms to extensively restoring valuable antique bears.

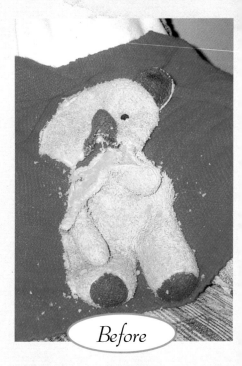

Before

After

This patient of Doc Pary's was all but destroyed by the owner's friend's dog. "He is a little lopsided and one ear is smaller than the other, but little by little, I was able to get most of the pieces back together," says Pary. The client, who had had the bear since birth, was thrilled.

Before

After

A puppy chewed the nose off this patient. He traveled to Doc Pary from South Carolina to get patched up.

MEET DOC PARY, PROVIDER OF BEAR CARE

After more than a decade of patching up tattered teddy bears, Paralee Schluchtner has become known to clients in her hometown near Denver, Colorado, and across the country (thanks to the Internet) as Doc Pary. Like most professional restoration artists, Doc Pary's work runs the gamut. She finds perfect matches to replace missing eyes. She resews detached arms and ears. She restuffs bears who have sagging padding. And, at times when critical care is called for, she fits together the puzzle pieces of bears that come to her as nothing but bags of scraps and parts.

Doc Pary is also a big believer in preventive medicine. Once a year, she holds a wellness clinic, inviting bear owners to bring their teddies in for annual checkups. ("I listen to their hearts and check their blood pressure, ears, height, weight, and eyes. The bears sometimes do need glasses.") She handles simple mending jobs on the spot for no cost. Owners of bears in need of more extensive "surgery" get cost estimates for the repairs. And no matter what, every bear gets the same prescription: "many hugs a day."

Doc Pary (with stethoscope) examining a bear at her annual wellness clinic

BEAR ESSENTIALS

These straight-shooting guys are here to remind you that elaborate, frilly looks aren't everything. *Enough embellishing this and accenting that, they say— with us, what you see is what you get.* If you want streamlined pieces of teddy bear art that are at home among the velvet throw pillows on your good sofa or atop the chenille spread on the guest bed, these are the minimalist teds you're looking for. Best of all, they're the easiest-to-make bears in the book.

DESIGNER:
BETH HILL

WHAT YOU NEED

Teddy Bear #1 Master Pattern, page 132

Teddy Bear #1 Master Instructions, page 40

Teddy Bear #1 Materials & Tools, page 40

ADDITIONS & ADAPTATIONS TO
MATERIALS & TOOLS

• Fabric: use any cotton fabric that features colors and a pattern that appeals to you

• Ribbon

INSTRUCTIONS

Follow the Teddy Bear #1 Master Instructions, then finish your bear by adding a ribbon around his neck. If you want to make a collection of these throw-pillow-style bears, experiment with shrinking or enlarging the pattern slightly to add size variation to your set.

BEAR FACTS

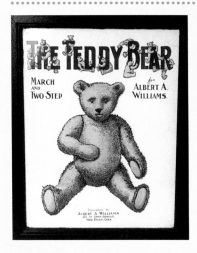

IN THE UNITED STATES BETWEEN 1907 AND 1911, MORE THAN 400 COPYRIGHTS WERE

REGISTERED FOR SONG TITLES USING THE WORDS TEDDY OR TEDDY BEAR.

MASTER INSTRUCTIONS

❧❧

TEDDY BEAR #2: NON-JOINTED BEAR

Pattern: page 133

MATERIALS & TOOLS

Fabric marker

Body fabric: ½ yard (.45 m) of either 45-inch (91 cm) or 58 to 60-inch (147 to 152 cm) fabric for a 17-inch (43.2 cm) bear (This yardage takes into consideration cutting for a nap or directional pattern, although it does not take into consideration any matching you might want to do for plaid or other print fabric. Use a ¼-inch [6 mm] seam allowance [already built into the pattern]. If your fabric is likely to fray, zigzag the edges of the pieces or apply fray retardant—especially to the edges of seams that will be closed by hand after you stuff your bear.)

Sharp scissors

Fray retardant

Color-headed pins and T-pins

Polyester sewing thread to match fabric

Upholstery thread, carpet thread, or cordonnet to match fabric

Stuffing

Stuffing stick

1 pair of eyes

#3 or #5 pearl cotton thread for embroidering facial features (optional on some bears)

Sewing machine or thread and needles

INSTRUCTIONS

1. Prepare the pattern, place the pieces on your fabric, mark them, and cut them out. Pay attention to the number you need of each piece, and note which pieces need to be cut facing each other. Transfer the guide markings to the fabric as well.

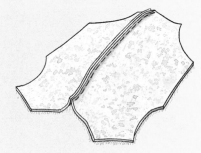

figure 1

2. Pin or baste the right sides of the body front together, then pin or baste the right sides of the body back together from the lower marking down. (The neck opening in the back should remain open at this point.) Stitch the front pieces together at the center body seam (figure 1) and the back pieces together at the back seam (figure 2).

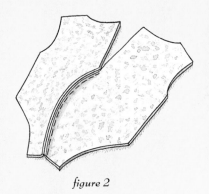

figure 2

figure 3

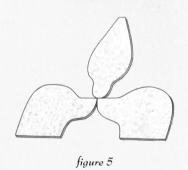

figure 4

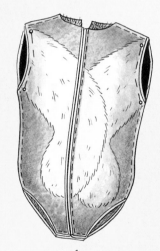

figure 5

3. Place the right sides of the stitched front body and back body together. Pin or baste the shoulder seams, side seams, and small, lower-body seam, then stitch them (figure 3). Leave the body inside out.

4. Pin or baste the right sides of the arm pieces and ears together, and stitch them. Pin or baste the right sides of the outer and inner legs together, and stitch them (figure 4).

5. To put your bear's head together, you'll fit the gusset between the two head pieces (figure 5 shows placement).

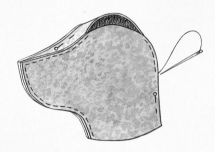

figure 6

6. Pin or baste the right sides of the head pieces together. Stitch from the nose (A on the pattern) to the neck edge (B on the pattern).

7. Pin or baste the head gusset into place, placing the center of the nose end of the gusset on the seam you

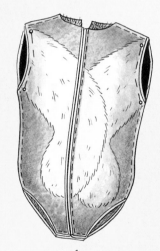

figure 7

sewed in step 6. Ease the gusset to fit as you pin or baste. Stitch the gusset into place, leaving one side of the head open at the markings (figure 6).

8. Carefully clip the seam allowance along the pattern's sharply curved lines (to make turning the bear right side out easier).

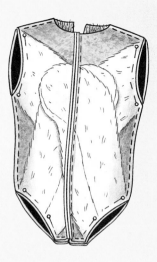

figure 8

9. Turn the arm and leg pieces right side out. Pin the arms into the openings on the body, matching the top arm seams to the top shoulder seams and the bottom arm seams to the side body seams (figure 7). Pin the legs into their body openings, matching the outer leg markings to the side body seams and the inner leg markings to the lower body seams (figure 8). When you finish, the legs and arms should be inside the body, with the right sides of limb and body material together. (Make sure the bear's feet point to the front of the body.) Because of the size of the openings, it's easiest to sew the arms and legs into place by hand, using a backstitch. However, you can use a machine stitch if you like.

10. Stitch closed the neck opening you left open in step 2 (the one between the top of the neck and the upper marking on your bear's back).

11. Turn the head right side out. Pin or baste the head to the body (with the head tucked inside the body, through the neck opening, like the limbs). Match the lower

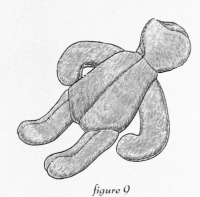

figure 9

head seam with the body front seam and the marking on the back of the gusset to the neck seam. Stitch the head into place either by hand or using a machine.

12. Turn the bear right side out through the back opening. You should now have an unstuffed "skin" (figure 9).

13. If you're using safety eyes and/or a safety nose, it's easiest to install them at this point. Approximate safety placement is noted on the gusset pattern piece. If you plan to embroider a nose, use button eyes, or create facial features in some other way, you're ready to stuff your bear.

14. Stuff each arm and leg to your desired fullness, leaving a small space between the body and arm or leg if you want your bear to sit and the arms to move a bit. Stuff the head, using a stuffing stick or a pencil to push the stuffing tightly into the nose area. Continue to stuff the head, making sure the nose area remains tightly stuffed. If you want a "huggable" feel to the body, stuff it moderately.

15. Add your bear's nose and mouth, working through either the head opening or the opening in the back. When you're finished, close the head opening using a ladder stitch and upholstery thread.

16. Add your bear's ears. Turn the ears right side out. Fold them under about ¼ inch (6 mm) around the ear opening, and pin or whipstitch the ears closed. Position the ears on the bear to your liking, pin them into position (T-pins work well for this), and whipstitch them into place with upholstery thread, making sure they're securely attached. Using a doll sculpture needle and going through the open back seam to sew the ears in place makes it easy to hide your thread knot and knot off when you're finished (figure 10).

17. Add your bear's eyes, again working through the back opening. Close the opening using a ladder stitch and upholstery thread when you're finished.

figure 10

AUTUMN TED

As if you couldn't guess from his spirited pose and that telltale baton, A.T. (as his friends call him) is a born leader. He was one of the first to arrive on the scene when we put out the call for teddy bears to help us celebrate their first 100 years, and he's been serving as ringleader, cheerleader, and all-around good guy since. When he's not helping organize bears for books, he leads hunts for wild acorns each fall—decked out in the acorn-gathering regalia he's wearing here.

DESIGNER
DEE DEE TRIPLETT

WHAT YOU NEED

Teddy Bear #2 Master Pattern, page 133

Autumn Ted Patterns, page 137

Teddy Bear #2 Master Instructions, page 58

Teddy Bear #2 Materials & Tools, page 58

ADDITIONS & ADAPTATIONS TO MATERIALS & TOOLS

• Body fabric: use 45-inch-wide (91 cm) cotton velveteen, ¼ yard (.25 m) golden yellow (legs), ⅓ yard (.3 m) orange (head, torso, and outer ears), and ¼ yard (.25 m) russet (arms and inner ears)

• ⅝-inch (1.6 cm) wooden dowel, 12 inches (30.5 cm) long

• 9 mm faceted black beads for the eyes (2)

• 5 mm faced black beads for the claws (20)

• Two pieces of contrasting colors of velveteen, each measuring approximately 4 x 21 inches (10.2 x 53.3 cm), for the leaves on the neck ruff

• ¼ yard (.25 m) fusible web for the neck ruff

• Dimensional paint in yellow and orange

• 18 inches (45.7 cm) of ½-inch (1.3 cm) grosgrain ribbon

• Oval wooden plaque, 8 x 10 inches (20.3 x 25.4 cm)

• Gesso

• Acrylic paints in colors that match body fabric

• Clear acrylic sealer

• 1½-inch (3.8 cm) wooden egg or acorn

• ⅛-inch (3 mm) wooden dowel, 12 inches (30.5 cm) long

• Iron

• Sandpaper

• Small paintbrush

INSTRUCTIONS

1.

Cut out your pieces as described in the Teddy Bear #2 Master Instructions, substituting the Autumn Ted Leg Pattern, page 137, and adding the Autumn Ted Tail Pattern, page 137. Instead of cutting all four ear pieces out of one color of fabric, cut two out of the orange head fabric and two out of the russet arm fabric, so you can make the inner ears and outer ears different colors.

2.

Sew the arms, head, and one leg as described in the Master Instructions.

You'll work on the second leg in step 4. (Note: when you're using non-fur fabric, such as the velveteen here, you may need to ease the head gusset to fit at the end of the nose, depending on the amount of give in your fabric.)

3.

Sew the torso, leaving the arm and head openings as described in the Master Instructions, but sewing closed the leg openings except for a small opening on one side, where you'll later insert the dowel to make your bear stand (see figure 1.)

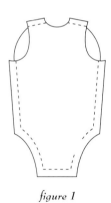

figure 1

4.

Sew the leg in which you'll be inserting the dowel, following the markings on the Autumn Ted Leg Pattern, which show an opening in the foot. Also, to help the leg fit the rounded bottom of the torso, trim the leg piece that will be the inner thigh, following the dotted line on the pattern. Turn the piece right side out.

5.

Stuff the toe of this foot, then insert the ⅝-inch (1.6 cm) dowel in the leg, pushing it through the hole in the foot until about ¾ inch (1.9 cm) protrudes. Stuff the rest of this leg very firmly.

6.

Turn the torso right side out, slide it down onto the dowel above the leg, and loosely stuff the torso (see figure 2).

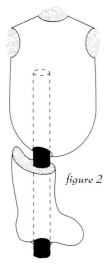

figure 2

7.

Turn the raw edge of the leg under, pin the top of the leg to the bottom of the torso, and finish stuffing the torso firmly. Ladder stitch the back opening on the torso closed.

8.

If necessary, adjust the pins on the top of the leg, making sure the join is neat and the bear is standing straight, then ladder stitch the leg in place, adding more stuffing, if you like, to make the leg firmer before sewing up the last inch.

9.

Turn the second leg and both arms right side out, stuff them, and attach them to the torso, following the same process. Press each stuffed limb to the torso and pin it in place with the raw edge turned under. Adjust the pins until the join is neat, then ladder stitch the limb in place, adding more stuffing, if necessary, before sewing up the last inch.

10.

Turn the head right side out, stuff it, and press it down into the neck. Tilt the head

at a jaunty angle, pin it in place, then ladder stitch it to the torso.

11.

Sew the ears, with the russet arm fabric serving as the inner ears, turn them right side out, and hand sew them to the head.

12.

Sew the tail, turn it right side out, and hand sew it to the bear's rear.

13.

Add the bear's facial features by stitching the larger black beads in place as eyes and embroidering the nose and mouth.

14.

For eyelashes, use two stands of pearl cotton thread to sew loops in a curve above the eyes, then clip the loops (see page 35).

15.

Sew five of the smaller black beads on the tip of each limb for claws

MAKING TED'S RUFF

1.

In addition to your two pieces of fabric for leaves, cut two more pieces, each measuring 4 by 21 inches (10.2 by 53.34 cm) from leftover body fabric for the backs of the leaves.

2.

Fuse each piece of leaf fabric to a piece of backing fabric, then from each piece, cut 10 leaves, using the Autumn Ted Leaf Ruff Pattern, page 137.

3.

Decorate each leaf with dimensional paint (or bead it, embroider it, or embellish it in some other way).

4.

Wrap the grosgrain ribbon around Ted's neck and mark it with pins where it meets.

Sew the leaves between the pins on the ribbon, overlapping each leaf about ¼ inch (6 mm), leaving tails of ribbon so that you can tie the ruff around Ted's neck.

PREPARING THE BASE

1.

Cover the wooden plaque with a coat of gesso, let it dry, then sand it until it's smooth.

2.

Paint the edge one color and the top another, then decorate the top with a painted pattern or with a stamped design.

3.

Once the paint is dry, add a coat of clear sealer.

4.

Drill a ⅝-inch (1.6 cm) hole in the plaque almost all the way through, then push the dowel extending from Ted's foot into the hole until he's standing on his own.

MAKING TED'S ACORN WAND

1. Drill a ⅛-inch (3 mm) hole in one end of a wooden egg, and insert the ⅛-inch (3 mm) dowel in the hole.

2. Paint the egg. When it's dry, use black dimensional paint to make small blobs that suggest an acorn cap. Apply clear sealer when the paint is dry.

3. Hand-sew the wand to Ted's hand.

TEDDY-MAKING TIP:

To play with positions for this bear's eyes and claws, use pins to temporarily place the beads before sewing them.

TEDDY BEARS WHO HELP MAKE IT ALL BETTER

T eddy bears have a corner on the comfort market. They're world-class experts when it comes to soothing, consoling, reassuring, and cheering up. Recognizing their natural caregiving gifts, some human beings (who happen to be pretty caring themselves) have mounted major efforts to get teddy bears into the arms of those who need them most.

A collection of Good Bears of the World

GOOD BEARS OF THE WORLD

Since 1969, the volunteer members of Good Bears of the World (who belong to "dens" around the globe) have been donating their official little bears to orphanages, women's shelters, hospitals, nursing homes, police and fire departments (who give them to traumatized young accident victims), and to victims of floods, earthquakes, and other natural disasters. Thousands of volunteers—including many teddy bear artists—help raise the money and handle the details of giving away tens of thousands of bears each year.

GULLIVER & GALIVANT: GOOD BEARS OF THE WORLD AMBASSADORS

In 1996, at the request of Good Bears of the World, renowned teddy bear artist Cindy Anschutz created Gulliver, who served as a traveling ambassador, spending three years circling the globe and spreading the word about the organization and its mission. His tour of duty ended with a celebration auction; he now resides at the site of the winning bidder, the Toy and Miniature Museum in Kansas City, Missouri. His sister, Galivant (also designed by Anschutz), has taken up the traveling where Gulliver left off.

Gulliver (above) and Galivant (left), the Good Bears of the World ambassadors

Sir Koff-A-Lot bears

SIR KOFF-A-LOT

Known for his excellent bedside manner, Sir Koff-A-Lot has spent decades functioning as an integral member of medical teams who treat patients recovering from invasive surgery. He was created by two cardiovascular surgeons (who also happened to be teddy bear collectors) to help patients with the respiratory therapy that's critical following open-heart surgery. Coughing and deep breathing are essential as therapeutic exercises after any invasive surgery (to help patients avoid complications such as pneumonia). But the actions are also uncomfortable, so many patients avoid them. Designed to serve as the perfect splint, Sir Koff-A-Lot (and his child-size version, Kiddie Kub) help absorb the pain of respiratory exercises—and provide a healing hug in the process.

Firefighters, police officers, and others who use Good Bears of the World to help calm young accident victims say the soft, cuddly teddies not only provide comfort, but they help break down barriers and make the uniformed officials seem less frightening.

HONEY

Do not confuse her with your average sort of bear who hangs around hives hoping for a taste of standard-issue honey. Oh no. Honey earned her reputation (not to mention her name) traveling around the world picking up designer pots of the very best honey high-end gourmet boutiques have to offer. Need to know where you might find an excellent avocado-blossom honey or a superior jar of creme d'honey? She's your source. Just remember that satisfying her highly developed palate keeps her extremely busy—it was a stroke of luck that we caught up with her here.

DESIGNER:

BETH HILL

WHAT YOU NEED

Teddy Bear #2 Master Pattern, page 133

Teddy Bear #2 Master Instructions, page 58

Teddy Bear #2 Materials & Tools, page 58

ADDITIONS & ADAPTATIONS TO MATERIALS & TOOLS

• Body fabric: use ½ yard (.45 m) blonde acrylic fur

• Ribbon

INSTRUCTIONS

Follow the Teddy Bear #2 Master Instructions, then finish your bear by adding a ribbon around her neck.

BEST-LOVED BEARS IN THE WORLD

▪ MARY'S BEAR ▪

Name: Bearly

Companion of Mary Since: 1950

Origin: The information is lost in the mists of family history.

Missing Features: Significant patches of fur (see Life-Altering Experience, below).

Life (and Look)-Altering Experience: Receiving a haircut by Mary, age 4, who decided, after she and her sisters had been to the beauty shop, that Bearly needed a trim, too. He's had to battle an unusual number of cowlicks since, but has never been altogether unhappy with his new look. Mary's mother, on the other hand, was not pleased.

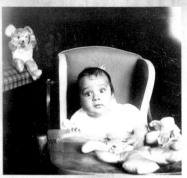

BEAR FACTS

Pandas and koalas, though cute and cuddly looking, aren't technically bears. China's giant panda is actually the largest member of the raccoon family, and Australia's koalas are marsupial mammals, who carry their young in a pouch.

TED D. ON SAFARI

Needless to say, Ted D.'s favorite part of this whole business of making a book about teddy bears was the photo shoot. It's the real reason he signed up at all. He loves to get out, go places. The more exotic and remote, the better. Unfortunately, since he is a teddy bear, he spends most of his time in quiet, safe, indoor spots. He makes up for it, though, by greeting every day dressed and adorned for adventure.

DESIGNER:
BARBARA BUSSOLARI

INSTRUCTIONS

Follow the Teddy Bear #2 Master Instructions, with a few additions and adjustments:

1.

Use yarn to sew beads to the fabric pieces before stitching the pieces together.

2.

Sew buttons and/or beads in place for the eyes. The eyes on the bear shown here were created by gluing beads onto buttons, then sewing the buttons to the face.

3.

Embroider the nose with the same yarn you used to attach the beads to the fabric.

4.

Stitch one arm and leg together to help Ted D. sit and to add to his character.

DECORATING THE FABRIC

Choose a fabric that already features a printed pattern, then embellish it with colored stamping.

1.

Cut your fabric approximately to size before stamping, so you don't end up stamping more than you need.

2.

Cover your work surface with scrap fabric or an old towel.

3.

Stamp, brush, or sponge fabric paint on randomly; no need at all for exactness.

Heat set the paint according to the manufacturer's instructions.

4.

Cut out your pieces, and check to make sure each one features some stamping. Don't be too fussy about equal coverage, though, or you'll ruin the appeal of this random look.

MAKING THE PAPER BEADS

These simple, handcrafted beads make your bear even more distinctive, but you can easily achieve a similar effect (and save a little time) by using purchased beads.

1.

Cut several pieces of commercial or handmade paper into small, tapered strips each approximately 2 inches (5.1 cm) long and ¼ inch (6 mm) wide. (Don't measure your strips exactly; as with the stamping, you're aiming for randomness over precision.)

2.

Roll each strip around a toothpick, then use a glue stick to hold the roll together.

3.

If you like, stick each toothpick with a bead wrapped around it into a piece of polystyrene foam, and, once you have a bunch lined up, spray them with clear paint. The paint gives the beads a little body, but this step isn't essential.

BEAR FACTS

IN ANCIENT CHINA, DREAMING OF A BEAR FORETOLD THE BIRTH OF A SON.

WHAT YOU NEED

Teddy Bear #2 Master Pattern, page 133

Teddy Bear #2 Master Instructions, page 58

Teddy Bear #2 Materials & Tools, page 58

ADDITIONS & ADAPTATIONS TO MATERIALS & TOOLS

• Body fabric: use pre-printed cotton fabric featuring an African-style design

• Fabric paint

• Stamps, brushes, or sponges

• Tapestry needle

• Yarn

• Interesting buttons and/or beads for the eyes

• Assortment of handmade or commercial papers

• Toothpicks

• Glue stick

• Polystyrene foam (optional)

• Fast-dry clear spray paint (optional)

HEIRLOOM BEAR

*S*ure, Heirloom Bear is cute. But the whole time the rest of us have been putting together this celebration of teddy bear history, she's been more than a little smug. See, combining teddy bears and the past is an idea she's been championing her whole life. She's known all along that people have warm, nostalgic feelings about teddy bears. Her idea has always been that they should take those feelings and build on them. *Make your bear out of materials that have sentimental value*, she says (grandma's handmade quilt, for example), *and you've got the most special bear in the whole world!* Did we mention how tiresome it is that Heirloom Bear is always right?

DESIGNER:

ELAINE MCPHERSON

WHAT YOU NEED

Teddy Bear #2 Master Pattern, page 133

Teddy Bear #2 Master Instructions, page 58

Teddy Bear #2 Materials & Tools, page 58

ADDITIONS & ADAPTATIONS TO MATERIALS & TOOLS

• Body fabric: use a passed-down family quilt or blanket or some other cherished piece of fabric

• Additional heirloom accents—anything with sentimental appeal (see list of starter suggestions below)

INSTRUCTIONS

Follow the Teddy Bear #2 Master Instructions, then embellish your bear with accents made from meaningful pieces. Here the designer has rolled rosebuds out of old silk and cut and hemmed a hole in a doily to create a lacy collar. She also glued on eyelids—just tiny half circles cut from the body fabric.

IDEAS FOR HEIRLOOM ACCENTS

Lace from a wedding dress

Pearls from a broken necklace

Ribbons

Buttons

Beads

Yarn

Fabric patches

BEST-LOVED BEARS IN THE WORLD

▪ BETH'S BEAR ▪

Name: T.K. (that's short for Teddy Cuddles)

Companion of Beth Since: 1947

Origin: Souvenir from parents' trip to New York City.

Missing Features: One ear, most fur, some of his excelsior stuffing—and his original nose is long gone.

Cosmetic Surgery He'll Admit To: The crocheted "cap" in the center of T.K.'s face represents his third nose job. Every time Beth, who slept nose-to-nose with Teddy Cuddles, nuzzled one away, her grandmother would crochet a new one. Beth still has her original nose, but says it's permanently creased.

Most Fulfilling Role: Muse. It was T.K. who first set Beth on a bearmaking path. Today, she sells handmade bears through her business, Bethbears—and she designed the master patterns and instructions, along with several of the project bears, for this book.

TEDDY-MAKING TIP:

You can make a number of bears out of a standard-size quilt or blanket. If you've got one that brings back vivid memories for the older generations in your family ("I remember that blue wool blanket was always at the foot of grandma and grandpa's bed"), you can use it to start a new tradition for the younger ones. Make bears for all the great-grandchildren, for example, and attach a tag to each that tells its history. It's a sure bet that the bears made out of blanket scraps—and their story—will be passed down for generations to come.

BEARLY THERE

Since the fabric he's made from could have (had the sewer had less imagination) easily been used to make an overcoat instead of a teddy bear, Bearly There feels awfully glad to be here. His chancy beginnings have also made him a big believer in lucky twists of fate. And this makes him a very agreeable bear. Rearrange plans in midstream, switch the schedule on him at the last minute, and he's happy with the change, convinced it means everything will turn out even better than it might have otherwise.

DESIGNER:
BETH HILL

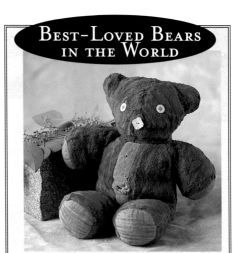

WHAT YOU NEED

Teddy Bear #2 Master Pattern, page 133

Teddy Bear #2 Master Instructions, page 58

Teddy Bear #2 Materials & Tools, page 58

ADDITIONS & ADAPTATIONS TO MATERIALS & TOOLS

• Body fabric: use ½ yard (.45 m) brown alpaca/wool coat fabric

• Ribbon

INSTRUCTIONS

Follow the Teddy Bear #2 Master Instructions, then finish your bear by adding a ribbon around his neck.

BEAR FACTS

BEARS PLAYED A MAJOR ROLE IN ANCIENT MYTHS OF NORTHERN ASIA AND NORTHERN NORTH AMERICA. THEY OFTEN APPEARED AS CREATURES WHO RESEMBLED HUMANS PHYSICALLY AND WERE CAPABLE OF BEGETTING HUMAN OFFSPRING.

BEST-LOVED BEARS IN THE WORLD

▪ TERRY'S BEAR ▪

Name: "He didn't have a name, he was just the bear who lived with 'Sleepy Bunny' at grandma's house."

Companion of Terry Since: 1953

Origin: Purchased by Terry's mother in Connecticut.

Missing Features: Original eyes and nose, buttons that once ran down his chest, some of his foam-rubber stuffing. The button eyes and nose Terry's Bear sports today are from Terry's grandma's sewing basket. Terry stitched them on himself when he was 12.

Longest Separation: Terry's Bear endured four years in storage in grandma's cellar while Terry and his family lived overseas. Terry rescued him when he returned home and hasn't parted with him since.

BEAR EAST

We've yet to determine whether Bear East is truly the most exotic bear in our bunch—or if he simply has the most active imagination and best storytelling skills. (Storytelling, you might want to be aware, is a common teddy bear talent.) We admit that his fine red silk and elegant black embroidery are convincing. The fact that he looks the part had a lot to do with our hanging on his every word as he told of his harrowing experience being left behind in a sleeping car on the Orient Express. (In a narrow escape, he was retrieved one stop later.) But it was his adventurous tales of weathering sandstorms and helping fight off raiding parties while traveling the Silk Road that started a few of us wondering. (*Do the math*, argued Theodore E. Bear, the book's fact checker—you'll meet him on page 94. *Teddy bears are just now 100 years old; the Silk Road disappeared centuries ago!*) Hmmmm…so it doesn't quite add up. Nevertheless, we decided it's more fun if Bear East never knows we're onto him.

DESIGNER:
MARY STANLEY CASADONTE

INSTRUCTIONS

1.

Cut out your pieces as described in the Teddy Bear #2 Master Instructions. Be sure to cut the gusset and head pieces out of velveteen. Also, cut two of the four ear pieces out of velveteen.

2.

Sew and stuff the bear, following the Teddy Bear #2 Master Instructions.

3.

Add the bear's facial features.

4.

Close up all the remaining openings, and attach the ears, making the red-fabric sides the inner ears (the ones facing forward when you look at the bear).

5.

Pin the piping in place (around the bear's neck, down the front, and around his waist, so it resembles the edges of a jacket), then hand-sew it on.

6.

Hand-sew the frogs in place, running down the bear's front, so they resemble closure clips on a jacket.

WHAT YOU NEED

Teddy Bear #2 Master Pattern, page 133

Teddy Bear #2 Master Instructions, page 58

Teddy Bear #2 Materials & Tools, page 58

ADDITIONS & ADAPTATIONS TO MATERIALS & TOOLS

• Body fabric: use ¼ yard (.25 m) of a silky red upholstery fabric with an Asian motif for the body and inner ears, and ¼ yard (.25 m) of velveteen in a complementary color for the head pieces and the outer ears.

• 1 yard (.9 m) thick black piping

• 3 black "frogs" (Asian jacket clips you can purchase, premade and in a variety of styles, at fabric stores)

BEAR FACTS

THE HERMANN COMPANY OF GERMANY LAYS CLAIM TO THE WORLD'S LARGEST TEDDY BEAR. MANUFACTURED IN 1952 (WHEN THIS SHOT WAS TAKEN), THEIR BIG BEAR MEASURES NEARLY 10 FEET (3 M) HIGH.

W

When teddy bears gather in any kind of group, they often organize a quick election and select one member to receive the most coveted teddy award of all: Cuddliest & Most Comforting. (It's their little way of celebrating a couple of the qualities teddy bears are best known for.) The bears who came together for this book were unanimous in naming Aromather-Bear their group's recipient. They cited his cozy polar fleece "fur," his humble blanket stitching, and his soft, snuggle-friendly features as obvious award-winning qualities. But what really impressed them is the fact that he's literally full of beans, beans that heat up during short spells he's willing to endure in a microwave oven. His warmed-up chest then activates an essential-oil-scented heart that ties in place on his front and gently helps induce sleep (if it's scented with chamomile), reduce stress (try drops of lavender), or provide any number of other herbal comforts.

DESIGNER:
KIM TIBBALS~ THOMPSON

AROMATHERAPY BEAR
(we call him Aromather-Bear for short)

INSTRUCTIONS

There's one primary difference between Aromather-Bear and other bears made following the Teddy Bear #2 Master Instructions. Instead of sewing him up with all of his right sides together and then turning him right side out, you sew him right side out to begin with, leaving the seam allowance visible, then blanket stitch over the allowance.

1.

Using both the Master Pattern and the Aromatherapy Bear Patterns, page 139, cut out your fabric pieces as described in the Teddy Bear #2 Master Instructions. Be sure to position the pattern pieces so the stretch of the fabric runs widthwise on the pieces, not lengthwise.

2.

Stitch all of the body pieces together, as described in steps 2 through 7 of the Teddy Bear #2 Master Instructions, with one overall exception: stitch the wrong sides rather than the right sides together. Also, don't leave the side opening in the head piece.

3.

Turn the arm and leg pieces wrong side out. Pin the arms into the openings on the body, matching the top arm seams to the top shoulder seams and the bottom arm seams to the side body seams. Pin the legs into their body openings, matching the outer leg markings to the side body seams and the inner leg markings to the lower body seams. When you finish, the legs and arms should be inside the body, with the wrong sides of limb and body material together. (Make sure the bear's feet point to the front of the body.)

WHAT YOU NEED

Teddy Bear #2 Master Pattern, page 133

Aromatherapy Bear Patterns, page 139

Teddy Bear #2 Master Instructions, page 58

Teddy Bear #2 Materials & Tools, page 58

ADDITIONS & ADAPTATIONS TO MATERIALS & TOOLS

• Body fabric: use ½ yard (.45 m) yellow polar fleece

• Piece of blue polar fleece, approximately 6 x 23 inches (15.2 x 58.4 cm), for inside ears, scarf, and heart

• Pieces of polar fleece in other colors, each 4 x 8 inches (10.2 x 20.3 cm), for additional hearts

• Scraps of green polar fleece for padding under nose and eyes

• Embroidery floss: 3 hanks of blue, 1 hank of yellow, 1 hank of green

• 24 inches (61 cm) blue satin ribbon ¼ inch (6 mm) wide

• 1½ lbs (approximately 660 g) small dry navy beans

• Assorted essential oils

• Glue gun and glue stick

4.

Stitch the arms and legs into place, then pull them back out of the body.

5.

Stitch closed the neck opening (the one between the top of the neck and the upper marking on your bear's back).

6.

Turn the head *wrong* side out. Pin or baste the head to the body (with the head tucked inside the body, through the neck opening, as you did with the limbs earlier). Match the lower head seam with the body front seam and the marking on the back of the gusset to the neck seam. Stitch the head into place, then pull the head out of the body. You should now have an unstuffed "skin."

7.

Trim all your seams to an even ⅛ inch (3 mm). With blue embroidery floss, overcast all the seams along the stitching, being careful to keep your stitch lengths even and to space your stitches equally.

8.

Stuff your bear as described in the Master Instructions, but substitute the dried beans for your other stuffing material when you stuff the main body cavity.

9.

Stitch the back seam closed, then overcast that seam area with blue embroidery floss.

10.

Cut nose and eye shapes out of green fleece, glue them in place, and then satin stitch over the templates with green embroidery floss.

11.

With blue embroidery floss, overcast the yellow ears along the stitching.

12.

Overcast the inside ears (the smaller blue pieces) with either yellow or green floss along the curved outer edges of each piece.

13.

Glue the inside ears to the larger ear pieces, keeping the bottom flat edges of all pieces even.

14.

Position the ears on your bear, and hand-sew them in place with yellow embroidery floss.

MAKING AROMATHER-BEAR'S SCARF

Simply overcast the edges of the blue scarf with either yellow or green embroidery floss, then tie the scarf around Aromather-Bear's neck.

MAKING AND ADDING AROMATHER-BEAR'S HEARTS

The idea here is that you can make a number of colored hearts, then dab each with a different essential-oil scent: rose oil on a pink heart, mint on a green heart, and so on.

1.

For each heart, pin the wrong sides together, insert a small satin ribbon loop inside the upper point of the heart, then stitch around the outside edges, leaving a small opening on one side.

2.

Stuff each heart, stitch the side opening closed, and overcast the seams with a contrasting color of embroidery floss.

3.

Fold a 10-inch (25.4 cm) strip of ribbon in half and crease it. At the crease, tack the ribbon to the upper left side of Aromather-Bear's chest.

4.

Thread the loop on one of the hearts through the ribbon on Aromather-Bear's chest, and tie the ribbon in a bow.

HOW TO USE AROMATHER-BEAR

1.

Place Aromather-Bear in a microwave oven, and heat him until the beans inside his body are toasty warm (about five to eight minutes).

2.

Scent one of the hearts with several drops of essential oil and tie it onto Aromather-Bear's chest. The heat from the beans will enhance the oil's scent for up to 45 minutes.

SCENT SUGGESTIONS

Lavender: for stress reduction

Rose: for sweet dreams

Chamomile: for calming and rest

Mint, Lemon, or Orange: for clarity of thought

Eucalyptus: to help you breathe easy; combine with rosemary, pine, or mint for an especially nice blend

* For a shot of this bear from behind, see page 58.

MATILDA'S GREAT ESCAPE

To tell you the truth, the other bears in the book weren't quite sure what to make of Matilda and her getup at first. Was she…? No, she couldn't be one of *them*. So then, maybe she was making fun of them? But she seemed to like teddy bears; why would she tease them? Turns out, as Matilda explained once she got to know everyone better, she loves teddy bears—more than many of the people she meets. So, on days when she'd rather not deal with any people at all, she nestles down into her teddy bear suit and goes about her business, enjoying the fact that no one ever disturbs her when she's dressed as her inner bear. And that seemed to make perfect sense to everybody.

DESIGNER:
TRICIA TUSA

WHAT YOU NEED

Teddy Bear #2 Master Pattern, page 133

Matilda's Great Escape Patterns, page 140

Teddy Bear #2 Master Instructions, page 58

Teddy Bear #2 Materials & Tools, page 58

ADDITIONS & ADAPTATIONS TO MATERIALS & TOOLS

• Body fabric: use ¾ yard (.7 m) brown velour, corduroy, flannel, or material from a thrift-store coat

• ¼ yard (.25 m) off-white cotton for pantalettes and scarf

• ½ yard (.45 m) flannel for dress

• ½ yard (.45 m) red felt for shoes

• Ribbon (one small piece of thick ribbon and another small piece of thin ribbon)

• 3 buttons for pantalettes and 2 buttons for the shoes

• Polymer clay for Matilda's head and features (approximately 2 squares of flesh-colored clay, one square of black, and small amounts of white and red)

• Toothpick

• Sharp pencil for head support

• Glue gun and glue sticks

INSTRUCTIONS

1.

Follow the Teddy Bear # 2 Master Instructions, but don't attach the bear's head. Instead, lightly stuff it, embroider its eyes, nose, and mouth, and sew up the head's side opening and the opening at its base, where it would typically attach to the body.

2.

Use the scarf piece of the Matilda's Great Escape Patterns (page 140) to cut a head scarf out of off-white cotton. Put the scarf around the bear's head and tie it on with the thicker ribbon.

3.

After adding all of the clothing (see the instructions below), secure the bear head in one of the arms with stitches here and there through the arm and into the head.

MAKING THE PANTALETTES

1.

Use the Matilda's Great Escape Patterns (page140) to cut your two pantalette pieces out of off-white cotton.

2.

Sew the two pieces together at the outside and inside of the legs. Hem the waistband and leg holes.

3.

Put the pantalettes on the bear body and fit them by gathering two pleats in the front and one in the back (following the markings on the pattern).

4.

Attach buttons at the top of each pleat.

MAKING THE DRESS

1.

Use the Matilda's Great Escape Patterns (page 140) to cut one skirt, one waistband, and one suspender strap out of flannel.

2.

Stitch the skirt side edges together, hem the bottom edge, and loosely stitch the top edge so you can pull one thread and create a gather.

3.

Fold the top edge of the waistband in ¼ inch (6 mm) toward the middle, and do the same with the bottom edge (see figure 1).

4.

Iron the top flap over the bottom flap (see figure 2). Fit the waistband over the gathered edge of the skirt, and sew it in place.

5.

Fold both edges of the suspender strap in approximately ¼ inch (6 mm), then fold the strap in half and press it. Top stitch along both edges of the folded strap. Stitch one end of the strap to the inside of the front of the waistband and the other to the inside of the back of the waistband. Add decorative buttons to the outside of the waistband at the points where the suspender strap attaches.

figure 1

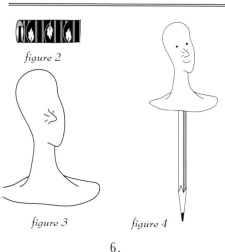

figure 2

figure 3   figure 4

6.

Slip the dress on the bear body, with the suspender strap over one shoulder.

MAKING THE SHOES

1.

Use the Matilda's Great Escape Patterns (page 140) to cut four shoe pieces and two shoe straps out of felt.

2.

For each shoe, hand stitch two pieces together, leaving the opening at the top where you'll slide in the bear's feet. If you like, add decorative stitching around those openings.

3.

Put the shoes on the bear's feet. Secure them by stitching a strap across the top of each, then add a decorative button where the strap meets the outside of each shoe, if you like.

MAKING MATILDA'S HEAD

1.

Skim the Polymer Clay Basics, below, before starting. Then, resurrect the Playdough-forming skills you likely mastered long ago to form a head and neck out of flesh-colored clay. Use your fingers to pinch features such as the nose, chin, and cheekbones into place, and a toothpick to create nostril holes. Create a base that fans out below the neck (see figure 3). You'll glue the bear fabric around the neck opening to this base later.

2.

Use tiny pieces of red, white, and black clay to add a mouth, eyes, and eyebrows.

3.

Stick a short, sharp pencil up through the neck area and into the head to create a deep hole.

4.

Form a floppy hat out of black clay. You'll bake the head and hat as separate pieces, then glue the hat in place later.

5.

Bake the pieces in a conventional oven, according to the directions on your polymer clay package, then remove them from the oven and let them cool completely.

6.

Using a glue gun, fill most of the hole in the base of the neck with glue, stick the pencil back in, and let the glue dry completely (see figure 4).

7.

Stick the head's pencil "post" through the body's neck hole and into the stuffing.

8.

Carefully apply a strip of glue from the glue gun along the edge of the clay base below the neck. Gently press the bear fabric around the neck hole onto the strip of glue to seal the neck area. Let the glue dry completely.

9.

Glue the hat onto the woman's head, and glue a bow (tied from the thin ribbon) to the hat, if you like.

POLYMER CLAY BASICS

This popular, easy-to-use, man-made material is sold in craft stores in small blocks or in bulk quantities, and comes in a wide range of bright, contemporary colors. Polymer clay is a combination of polyvinyl chloride (PVC), plasticizer, and color pigments. It's as pliable as ceramic clay in its initial state. Once you've molded and sculpted it into shape, you simply "fire" it in a standard oven to harden it.

Even the softest brands of polymer clay are a bit stiff right out of the package, so you'll want to condition yours before working with it. Starting with a small amount, warm the clay in your hand or wrap it in wax paper and then a towel and place it on a sunny windowsill. Once it's pliable, roll the clay into a ball, then into a log. Stretch out the log, then fold it back on itself. Continue twisting and rolling the clay until it's an even consistency and color. Once it's conditioned, you can roll your polymer clay into a ball, wrap it in plastic, and store it in a cool, dry place for up to a week before using it.

Polymer clay is certified nontoxic, but it's a good idea to take a few precautions to minimize exposure to its chemical ingredients.

· Don't use kitchen utensils to prepare food once you've used them to manipulate polymer clay.

· Bake your polymer clay objects in a well-ventilated area, and clean the inside surfaces of your oven thoroughly with baking soda and water afterward.

· Wear rubber gloves while working with the clay, or wash your hands well afterward.

THE BIG BEAR MARKET

The craze for teddy bears themselves quickly created a burgeoning market for all sorts of bear-related memorabilia. Shortly after teddies hit the scene in 1902, bear lovers could round out their worlds with novelty items ranging from brass teddy bear buttons and silver teddy bear baby spoons to teddy bear jumping jacks, jewelry, hand muffs, perfume bottles, and teething rings. Soon, people were also reading tall teddy bear tales, playing teddy bear board games, eating off of teddy bear china, and tapping their toes to popular teddy tunes.

Porcelain toothpick holder featuring "Teddy and the Bear"

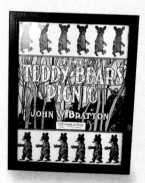

Teddy Bears were gifted with their very own anthem in 1907, when John W. Bratton wrote the popular instrumental piece, *The Teddy Bears Picnic*. In 1930, songwriter Jimmy Kennedy added lyrics to the melody, and people haven't stopped singing the teddy bear's praises since.

In 1905, author Seymour Eaton added to the teddy bear's rapidly growing appeal with the creation of his popular storybook characters, Teddy B and Teddy G, the Roosevelt Bears. They first starred in rhyming tales published in leading newspapers across the United States. Then, in 1906, Eaton published *The Roosevelt Bears, Their Travels and Adventures*, the first in a series of much-loved books.

An early Ideal Novelty and Toy Company teddy bear pictured with *The Three Baby Bears* (1907), from the Little Mother's series, and a tin pail decorated with teddy bears playing in a band, circa 1907.

Cards from the "Game of Teddy Bear,"
created in 1907

A tin lithograph Roosevelt bear riding a tricycle, manufactured in 1907

An assortment of Roosevelt Bear china, manufactured in 1908

China from the "Teddy and Rosa" series, manufactured circa 1908

MASTER INSTRUCTIONS

TEDDY BEAR #3: JOINTED BEAR

Pattern: page 134

MATERIALS & TOOLS

Fabric marker

½ yard (.45 m) of either 45-inch (91 cm) or 58 to 60-inch (147 to 152 cm) fabric for a 17-inch (43.2 cm) bear (This yardage takes into consideration cutting for a nap or directional pattern, although it does not take into consideration any matching you might want to do for plaid or other print fabric. Use a ¼-inch [6 mm] seam allowance [which is already built into the pattern]. If your fabric is likely to fray, zigzag the edges of the pieces or apply fray retardant—especially to the edges of seams that you'll close by hand after you stuff your bear.)

Sharp scissors

Fray retardant

Felt square or ultrasuede square (or other paw pad material)

Color-headed pins and T-pins

Polyester sewing thread to match fabric

Upholstery thread, carpet thread, or cordonnet to match fabric

Joint system of choice and tools for installing the joints
(See Jointing Systems, page 20.)

Stuffing

Stuffing stick

1 pair of eyes

#3 or #5 pearl cotton thread for embroidering facial features (optional on some bears)

Pet brush (optional)

Sewing machine or thread and needles

INSTRUCTIONS

1.

Prepare your pattern and transfer it, along with all markings, to your material. Cut out the pieces of the bear. In addition to marked openings, your pieces should have joint markings on the inner arm pieces and on the two facing leg pieces (the ones that will be the inner legs).

2.

On all pattern pieces with marked openings, either use a tight, small zigzag stitch along the opening edges or apply fray retardant.

3.

Sew the straight ends of the paw pads to the straight ends of the inner arms, right sides together (figure 1).

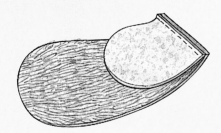

figure 1

4.

Pin or baste all the individual parts together, right sides facing (figure 2).

5.

Begin stitching the parts together, using a ¼-inch (6 mm) seam allowance (which has already been added to the pattern). Stitch the arms and legs first, and set them aside. Be sure to leave the bottom of the feet open on each leg, so you can insert foot pads later.

6.

Stitch the front body seam, then stitch the back body seam from the marking at the neck, leaving the center back open between the markings. Stitch the front body to the back body, leaving small openings for joint insertion as marked (figure 3). Apply fray retardant over the joint openings. You might also want to mark each opening with a big loop of thread that shows through on the fabric's right side, so you can easily find the openings later when you're installing the joints. Set the pieces aside.

figure 2

7.

To put your bear's head together, you'll fit the gusset between the two head pieces (see figure 5, page 59). Pin or baste the right sides of the head pieces together. Stitch from the nose (A on the pattern) to the neck edge (B on the pattern).

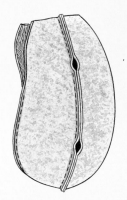

figure 3

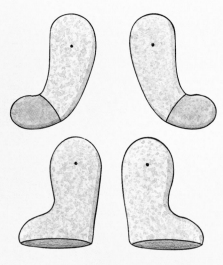

figure 4

8.

Pin or baste the head gusset into place, positioning the center of the nose end of the gusset on the seam you sewed in step 7. Ease the gusset to fit as you pin or baste. Stitch the gusset into place, leaving one side of the head open at the markings (see figure 6, page 59).

9.

Insert the foot pads into the openings you left in the feet in step 5, and pin or baste them in place. Match one of the foot-pad markings to the leg's toe seam and the other to the heel seam. Stitch them in place by hand or machine, easing them to fit. (Hand-sewing is easiest if you're working with bulky fabric.)

10.

Stitch the ears together.

11.

Carefully clip the seam allowance along the pattern's sharply curved lines (to make turning the bear right side out easier).

12.

Turn the head right side out. If you're working with fur, trim ¼ inch (6 mm) of fur from the neck edge, and zigzag stitch around the edge or apply fray retardant.

13.

Pierce the inside legs and inner arms with an awl to make places for inserting the joints, following the markings on the pattern. Pierce the pieces carefully, making sure you're piercing through only one layer of fabric, then apply fray retardant over the holes. (Again, you may want to mark each hole with a big loop of thread that shows through on the fabric's right side, so you can easily find the holes later when you're installing the joints.) Also, be sure the toes on the two legs are pointing in opposite directions (rather than in the same direction) when you mark the holes, so both feet will face forward when you attach the legs (figure 4). Turn the body, legs, arms, and ears right side out.

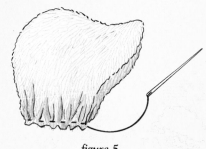

figure 5

14.

Using carpet thread or cordonnet and a gathering stitch, gather the neck opening of the head piece closed and secure (figure 5, page 85). Joint the head to the neck of the body and joint the legs and arms to the body (see Adding Joints, page 25). You should now have an unstuffed "skin" (figure 6).

15.

If you are using a "safety" or plastic nose, make a hole in the muzzle center and install it at this point, working through the opening in the head. You should also install safety eyes at this point, at about the indentation of the muzzle and head.

16.

Stuff the head. Use small pieces of stuffing, beginning with the muzzle area. Pack the stuffing tightly with a stuffing stick. After the muzzle area, stuff the remainder of the head. In most cases, it's best to tightly stuff the head, even if you wish to lightly stuff the body, arms, and legs. A tightly stuffed muzzle will make it easier to embroider a nose, if you choose to do so.

17.

Add your bear's nose and mouth, working through the head opening. When you're finished, close the opening using cordonnet or carpet thread and a ladder stitch.

18.

Stuff the remainder of the bear and close all remaining openings with cordonnet or carpet thread and a ladder stitch.

19.

Add your bear's ears. Turn the ears right side out. Fold them under about ¼ inch (6 mm) around the ear opening, and pin or whipstitch the ears closed. Position the ears on the bear to your liking, pin them into position (T-pins work well for this), and whipstitch them into place with upholstery thread, making sure they're securely attached. If you're working with a long doll sculpture needle, you can angle the needle down to the neck joint area, where you can come out and knot off.

20.

Add your bear's eyes, coming out and knotting off in the neck joint area, as you did above.

21.

Use a pet brush or the tip of a needle to tease out any fur trapped in seams. If you wish, trim around the eyes and mouth, so the features are more visible, or trim off the fur from the entire muzzle. If you trim the muzzle, work carefully with sharp-pointed scissors until you achieve the desired effect.

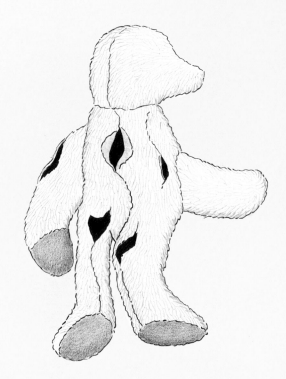

figure 6

TEDDY CARE TIPS

• A clean bear will typically enjoy a longer life than a grubby one. You can surface wash most teddy bear fabrics (except for velveteen, felt, and cotton plush) with the foam of a mild liquid detergent dissolved in cool water. Use the foam to get rid of surface dust and static, then wipe the bear with a clean, damp washcloth. Be sure to dry your bear completely afterward, or he'll be in danger of molding and rotting. Fluffy terry cloth towels are best at absorbing moisture. Use white ones; the dye in colored towels might bleed onto your bear.

• Machine washing will destroy the joints in a jointed bear, but unjointed bears made from synthetic materials can usually be laundered by machine. To avoid excess wear and tear, though, skip the dryer. Put your bear in a mesh bag, and hang him from the clothesline.

• To remove loose dust from a teddy bear's fur before cleaning or washing him, use a bristle brush. If the fabric is especially fragile, try a baby's brush or comb instead. And for surface cleaning unwashable bear fabrics, try a suede brush.

• If you're packing up a bear for storage, brown paper tied with string will do the best job of letting your bear breathe and allowing moisture to evaporate. Shoe boxes are also good options for smaller bears. Wrap any bear that's especially fragile in acid-free tissue paper before boxing it up. Use plastic bags only for temporary storage—or for temporarily sealing up a moth-eaten bear with mothballs, to kill the insects.

BEST-LOVED BEARS IN THE WORLD

▪ BRIAN'S BEAR ▪

Name: Sam

Companion of Brian Since: 1971

Origin: Made by Brian's mother's friend Vesta.

Missing Features: Nose, mouth, and tongue (which once stuck out of mouth).

Most Traumatic Experience: Regular episodes of hanging by his ears from the clothesline after being subjected to a spin in the washing machine. Seeing Sam suspended from the clothesline was also traumatic for Brian, who, the story goes, responded by running through the yard screaming.

HOMER

With his traditional cotter-pin joints, his reproduction shoe-button eyes, and his classic mohair fur, Homer is, without a doubt, this group's venerable elder statesman. His response to the nontraditional fabrics and innovative styles other bears in the book have trotted out is a gentle and kindly smile. He's not at all opposed to modern trends in teddy bear design, he says, just wise enough to know that a classic look works best for him.

DESIGNER:
BETH HILL

WHAT YOU NEED

Teddy Bear #3 Master Pattern, page 134

Teddy Bear #3 Master Instructions, page 84

Teddy Bear #3 Materials & Tools, page 84

ADDITIONS & ADAPTATIONS TO MATERIALS & TOOLS

• Body fabric: use ½ yard (.45 m) curly and matted mohair

• Fabric for paw and foot pads: use Ultrasuede

• Ribbon

INSTRUCTIONS

Follow the Teddy Bear #3 Master Instructions, then finish your bear by adding a ribbon around his neck.

BEAR FACTS

A.A. MILNE'S WINNIE THE POOH BOOKS HAVE BEEN TRANSLATED INTO 22 LANGUAGES, INCLUDING LATIN AND ESPERANTO (AN ARTIFICIAL INTERNATIONAL LANGUAGE BASED ON WORDS COMMON TO THE CHIEF EUROPEAN LANGUAGES).

BEST-LOVED BEARS IN THE WORLD

▪ DIANA'S BEAR ▪

Name: "I got him when I was just born, so I was too busy to think up a name."

Companion of Diana Since: 1967

Origin: Made by the Commonwealth Toy Company of Brooklyn, New York. Purchased by Diana's parents in Arlington, Virginia.

Missing Features: A little worn (and in the case of the nose and mouth, smushed into a new position), but he's got them all!

Proudest Distinction: Claims the title of "Diana's First Stuffed Animal Ever."

BUMBLEBEAR

Bumblebear is the kind of bear you want to take under your wing. He's forever stumbling his way into one blunder or another, but always with good humor and the best of intentions. In his eagerness to please, he's been known to overturn camera equipment, upend light stands, and spill steaming cups of tea over hot-off-the-press book proofs. Bumblebear is also incredibly trusting, which doesn't always work to his advantage. Still, it's hard not to love the fact that he's inclined to see all fellow creatures as potential playmates.

DESIGNER:
**MARY STANLEY
CASADONTE**

WHAT YOU NEED

Teddy Bear #3 Master Pattern, page 134

Teddy Bear #3 Master Instructions, page 84

Teddy Bear #3 Materials & Tools, page 84

ADDITIONS & ADAPTATIONS TO MATERIALS & TOOLS

• Body fabric: ¼ yard (.25 m) fabric featuring a bumblebee pattern for the body and inner ears, and ¼ yard (.25 m) velveteen in a complementary color for the head pieces and the outer ears.

• 10 inches (25.4 cm) decorative piping

• Paw & foot pad fabric: use ¼ yard (.25 m) of the same velveteen you're using for the head and outer ears

• Scrap of pink felt for tongue

• Plastic nose

• Decorative bee (available at craft stores)

INSTRUCTIONS

1.

Cut out your pieces as described in the Teddy Bear #3 Master Instructions. Be sure to cut the gusset and head pieces out of the velveteen. Also, cut two of the four ear pieces out of velveteen.

2.

Sew and stuff the bear, following the Teddy Bear #3 Master Instructions. When you sew the ears, use the bumblebee pieces for the inner ears (the parts of the ears that will face forward).

3.

Add the bear's facial features, embroidering his eyes so they're crossed (they'll later appear to be focused on the bee you'll attach to his nose). Cut a tongue out of the pink felt, and stitch it in place, so it sticks out of one side of his mouth.

4.

Close up all the remaining openings.

5.

Sew a strip of piping around the inner-ear border of each ear, then attach the ears.

6.

Embroider claws on the paws and food pads.

7.

Appliqué the pads onto the feet.

8.

Use a thin piece of wire to attach the bee to your bear's nose.

THIS IS IT, JUST ONE MORE...

Japanese collector Yoshihiro Sekiguchi has so many teddy bears, he founded three museums to display his constantly growing collection. He's pictured here with "Teddy Girl," a rare 1904 Steiff bear, for which he paid a record-breaking price.

THE TEDDY BEAR COLLECTING CRAZE

If you're under the impression that a teddy bear is something you receive one of at a young age and then cross off your list of life's must-have possessions, have you got a lot to learn. And you'd better get busy. While others were fiddling with stamps and rare books, teddy enthusiasts have built bear collecting into a huge international hobby.

Fortunately for the would-be collector who wants to get up to speed fast, the teddy bear world, as you might imagine, is one that's big and friendly. It's full of teddy bear clubs (some have their own teddy festivals complete with teddy queens), teddy bear artist groups, teddy bear websites and chat rooms, teddy bear newsletters, teddy bear magazines published around the world, teddy bear museums, and (best of all, according to active collectors) teddy bear conventions, where you can connect with artists, manufacturers, dealers, and fellow fans all at once.

Bear collectors are as varied in their approaches as the bears they add to their display shelves. Some collect nothing but modern manufactured bears. Others only antiques. Some travel to dozens of shows every year. Others trade bears from the comfort of their home computers. And while all teddy bear collectors will tell you they do what they do first and foremost for love, some also invest big money. Top auction houses including Sotheby's, Christie's, and Phillips all cater to teddy bear connoisseurs who love the thrill of high-price bidding. Hundreds, including growing numbers of newcomers, pack the salesrooms and light up the phone lines at each auction, vying for bears that have been fetching record six-figure hammer prices. It's all proof, say auction-house officials, that the bear market is only getting bigger.

COLLECTION CATEGORIES

If the number of square feet you can devote to your teddy bear collection is limited, you may want to narrow your focus just a bit. Here are some categories you might consider collecting by.

• Manufactured bears

• Handmade artist bears

• Antique bears

A collection of bears on display at the Izu Museum an hour outside of Tokyo, Japan

- *Bears you've made yourself*

- *Bears made the year you were born*

- *Bears that are a single color (all blue bears, maybe)*

- *Bears made by a single manufacturer (Steiff, for example)*

- *Miniature bears*

- *Limited-edition reproduction bears*

- *Character bears (Yogi Bear, say, and his cartoon-bear counterparts)*

- *Bears that come with photos of themselves with their original owners*

DISPLAYING YOUR TEDDY BEAR COLLECTION

- *Group your bears by color*

- *Group your bears by type (Put all the pandas together on one shelf, for example.)*

- *Position them on dolls' or children's furniture, such as benches, rockers, and chairs*

- *Arrange them on antique toys, including sleds, rocking horses, trains, and large wooden blocks*

- *Create tiny vignettes with your bears— tea parties, reading groups, and the like*

BEAR FACTS

It's a formal-sounding name for such a cozy hobby, but a collector or lover of teddy bears is known by people who know such things as an arctophile. That's ARK-tuh-fyl, from the Greek words for bear (arctos) and love (philos).

THEODORE E. BEAR

Any group that wants to accomplish something needs a member who keeps the others on task. (Many book editors, it should be pointed out, also benefit from having a taskmaster nearby.) Theodore E. Bear has been ours—and he's not only kept us on schedule, he's kept us honest. In addition to being a stickler about deadlines, he's fastidious when it comes to facts. (Just ask any other bear in the book, he's got them all, whether they have to do with stitching techniques or teddy bear trivia.) With one eye on the calendar and the other on a stack of reference books, Theodore E. Bear, perpetually dressed for the start of the fall semester, helped us all make the grade.

DESIGNER:
TERRY TAYLOR

WHAT YOU NEED

Teddy Bear #3 Master Pattern, page 134

Theodore E. Bear Leaf Patch Pattern, page 138

Teddy Bear #3 Master Instructions, page 84

Teddy Bear #3 Materials & Tools, page 84

ADDITIONS & ADAPTATIONS TO MATERIALS & TOOLS

• Body fabric: use a slightly nubby upholstery fabric with a subtle pattern

• Fabric for paw and foot pads: use Ultrasuede in a color that picks up one of the accent colors in your body fabric (You'll need enough Ultrasuede to also cut out two of the ear pieces and the small leaf patch.)

• #6 knitting needles and medium-weight knitting worsted in two colors (if you want to knit your own scarf)

INSTRUCTIONS

1.

Cut out your pieces as described in the Teddy Bear #3 Master Instructions. Cut two of the four ear pieces out of the Ultrasuede you're using for paw and foot pads and two out of the body fabric.

2.

Sew the bear, following the Teddy Bear #3 Master Instructions. When you sew the ears, use the ultrasuede pieces for the inner ears (the parts of the ears that will face forward).

3.

Using the Theodore E. Bear Leaf Patch Pattern, page 138, mark and cut the patch out of Ultrasuede. Before stuffing the bear, pin the patch in place on the bear's chest, and slip stitch it on.

4.

Stuff and finish the bear, following the Teddy Bear #3 Master Instructions.

KNITTING THEODORE E. BEAR'S SCARF

If you're a knitter, you'll be able to whip up this simple scarf in no time. If not, make it easy on yourself and purchase a scarf meant for a doll.

1.

Cast on 18 stitches. Knit with a stockinette stitch throughout.

2.

Knit two rows in one color, then 10 rows in second color. Repeat the pattern until your scarf is as long as you want it. End with a small, two-row stripe.

3.

Add fringe to each end if you like.

■ SANDI'S BEAR ■

Name: Sally

Companion of Sandi Since: 1953

Origin: Christmas gift from Grandma and Grandpa Stambaugh. (Sisters Jane and Joy received identical bears.)

Distinguishing Characteristic: Often smelled not so faintly of "Evening in Paris" (Sandi's mother's perfume), which Sandi applied to Sally regularly so she could be sure to tell her apart from her sisters' bears.

Show of Endurance: Out-surviving Jane's and Joy's bears. "Three marriages and a million moves later, I've still got her!"

BIG-NAME BEARS

WINNIE THE POOH

One of the biggest names of all when it comes to bears is Winnie the Pooh, the pudgy little star of books, radio shows, and Disney films, whose devotees revere him as everything from best friend to philosopher. Pooh started out as a real teddy bear, sitting on the shelves of London's Harrods department store. He was purchased in 1921 by Dorothy Milne, wife of author Alan Alexander Milne, for their son Christopher Robin's first birthday. At first, he was called Edward Bear, but within a few years, he had assumed his more famous and lasting name. It came from Winnie, an American black bear, mascot of a Canadian regiment from Winnipeg, who Christopher Robin loved to visit at the London Zoo, and Pooh, after Christopher Robin's favorite swan.

The original Winnie the Pooh, purchased in London in 1921 by Dorothy Milne, wife of author A.A. Milne and mother of Christopher Robin

Pooh first appeared (as Edward Bear) in A. A. Milne's book of verse, When We Were Very Young, in 1924. He then inspired his namesake Winnie The Pooh, published two years later. Artist Earnest Howard Shepard created the original pencil-drawn Pooh Bear, basing his illustrations in part on his own son's Steiff teddy bear. When the Walt Disney Studios began producing musical Winnie the Pooh cartoon features in the mid-1960s, a new generation of fans fell in love with a plumper, colorful Pooh who spoke with an American accent and wore a red T-shirt. In addition to mass distribution of Pooh films and paraphernalia, Winnie The Pooh itself has sold millions of copies in 22 languages, making this "silly old bear" perhaps the best-known bear in the world.

BIG-NAME BEARS

SMOKEY BEAR

It's hard to find a story more sentimental than Smokey's. Invented as a symbol for the U.S. Forest Fire Prevention Campaign, the first Smokey Bear image appeared on a poster in 1944, along with his slogan: "Only you can prevent forest fires." But his popularity soared in the 1950s, when he took the form of a real, live bear cub who narrowly escaped a tragic blaze in New Mexico's Lincoln National Forest. Firefighters told of finding the scared and hungry cub clinging to the charred remains of a tree he had climbed to escape the terrible blaze. Impressed by his bravery, they made him their mascot, entrusted him with the name of Smokey, and sent him to the National Zoo in Washington, D.C., where he was nursed back to health and lived out the rest of his life enjoying visits from thousands of young fans.

Saturday Evening Post illustrator Albert Staehle created the first Smokey Bear image—an undressed bear putting out a campfire with a bucket of water. Later, he was given denim jeans, a ranger hat, and his own address, so Junior Forest Rangers could be in touch with him. In 1952, the United States Congress passed the Smokey Bear Act, which ensured that only the U.S. Department of State Foresters and the Advertising Council could license the manufacture of Smokey products. That meant proceeds from the sales of Smokey Bear binoculars, hats, figurines, comic books, stuffed toys, and other memorabilia—early versions of which are all highly collectible today—would forever help fund the prevention of forest fires.

BIG-NAME BEARS

RUPERT BEAR

Rupert Bear made his debut in November 1920 on the pages of Britain's Daily Express. *He continues to star today in one of the longest-running children's newspaper cartoons ever—and his appeal has become universal.*

Children's book illustrator Mary Tourtel created Rupert at the request of her husband, a Daily Express editor who was searching for a cartoon that could compete with the Daily Mail's Teddy Tail *and Daily Mirror's* Pip, Squeak, and Wilfred. *Tourtel, who both drew and wrote the Rupert Bear strip until her eyesight failed in 1935, situated her boy-like bear in the enchanting world of Nutwood, where his natural curiosity led him on adventurous encounters with the likes of fairies, magicians, and dragons. Alfred Bestall took over the strip for the next 30 years. He helped refine Rupert's look and modernize his escapades, all the while sticking to Rupert's standard and endearing story line: one of an idealistic young bear venturing out to explore the wider world, then returning safely home.*

Courtesy of The Bear Museum, Petersfield, Hampshire, United Kingdom

The Rupert Annual, *a yearly collection of Rupert cartoons, is a popular holiday-season tradition that began in 1936. In addition, Rupert has appeared in animated television series and on video tape and has been sold in the form of everything from puzzles to puppets—and, of course, stuffed toys. His hard-core fans are members of Followers of Rupert, a decades-old worldwide organization dedicated to maintaining the purity of his tradition.*

BIG-NAME BEARS

PADDINGTON BEAR

Paddington Bear appeared on the scene in London, England, in 1958—straight "from Darkest Peru." He came with his characteristic duffle coat, floppy hat, and suitcase (his wellington boots were added to illustrations later, then worked into the Paddington stories by his creator, author Michael Bond). Paddington Bear also came with an endearing fondness for fun and adventure—which, to the delight of his readers, meant Paddington was seldom far from imminent disaster, whether he was attempting to take a bath or make a batch of dumplings.

Building on the resounding success of the first Paddington book, A Bear Called Paddington, Bond, who had based the character on a teddy bear he'd purchased for his wife, published a new Paddington book each year until 1966, followed by six new collections of stories between 1968 and 1981. Paddington gained world renown in 1975, when his stories were transformed into an animated puppet series, originally shown on British television. Artist Peggy Fortnum created the original Paddington illustrations; other artists later drew their own versions of the mischievous little bear, whose likeness has appeared on everything from bicycle bells to chocolates.

RARE BEARS

All teddy bears are special, of course. But in the world of high-dollar teddy collecting, some have achieved outright celebrity status. Like other coveted collectibles, they've gained fame for their fascinating histories, their singular or limited-edition status, and because of the people who made them or owned them before. Here's a sampling of some of the most novel and sought-after bears.

TEDDY EDWARD

Touted as one of the world's most-traveled bears, Teddy Edward, circa 1950, accompanied his original owner, Patrick Matthews, on adventures involving everything from sailboats and climbing gear to snow skis and jeeps. Patrick's wife, Mollie, wrote a series of stories to accompany the photographs Patrick took of Teddy Edward's escapades. They evolved into a collection of books and a popular British Broadcasting Corporation series, Watch with Mother.

BERLIN WALL BEAR

This limited-edition bear was manufactured by Hermann in 1990 to celebrate German reunification. He packs a little piece of the Berlin Wall inside his rucksack.

Teddy Edward

GATTI

He's only 6 inches (15.2 cm) tall, but Gatti is a stalwart little bear. He belonged to Gaspare Gatti, catering manager of the Titanic and one of the victims of the ship's 1912 disaster. Mr. Gatti's tiny bear—completely unharmed—was one of his few possessions recovered from the tragedy. Later, during the bombing raids over London during World War II, the bear again narrowly escaped damage.

Berlin Wall Bear

MR. WHOPPIT

This representative of a line of bears created by the Merrythought toy company in the mid-1950s has led a fast-paced life. His owner, Donald Campbell, broke numerous world speed records on both land and water, many with Mr. Whoppit in tow. Campbell's body was never recovered when he was killed in a water race in 1967, but rescue workers did find Mr. Whoppit floating on the surface.

ALFONZO

In 1908, George Mikhailovich, the Grand Duke of Russia, commissioned Steiff to make Alfonzo, a rare rust-red mohair bear, for his daughter, Princess Xenia Georgievna. The Princess took the bear with her on a 1914 trip to visit royal relatives at Buckingham Palace in England, unaware that she and her bear would never return home. With the outbreak of World War I, both were detained in England, a twist of fate that saved the Princess from certain death in the Russian Revolution. Alfonzo, who represented her homeland and her beloved father, became her prized possession.

HORATIO

Made in Germany around 1910, this golden mohair bear comes with his very own ghost. He was owned by a sea captain, Thomas Milligan, until Milligan's death in 1951. But, so the stories go, Horatio is seldom without his longtime companion. Milligan's ghost has frequently been spotted with the bear, and when Horatio is in the room, it's said the scent of the old sea captain's tobacco fills the air.

GALLERY OF TEDDY BEARS

Edie Barlishen. Bailey, 17″ (43.2 cm), 1998. Mohair, Ultrasuede paws, glass eyes, plastic-pellet and polyester stuffing, vintage baby sweater. Photo by artist

Mary Lou Foley. Tallicut and Her Cub, 8″ x 5″ x 14″ (20.3 x 12.7 x 35.6 cm), 2000. German mohair, glass eyes. Photo by artist

Kathlyn Gordon. Denim, 3″ (7.6 cm), 1999. Denim fabric, onyx eyes, polyester and glass-pellet stuffing, silk ribbon. Photo by artist

Loris Hancock. Realistic Pandas, baby: 4″ x 2″ x 1¾″ (10.2 x 5.1 x 4.4 cm), reclining bear: 6″ x 4″ x 3″ (15.2 x 10.2 x 7.6 cm), standing bear: 2¾″ x 3″ x 6″ (7 x 7.6 x 15.2 cm), 2000. Alpaca, glove-leather nose, Ultrasuede paws. Photo by artist

Edie Barlishen. Kobi, 1¾″ (4.4 cm), 1999. Upholstery velvet, Ultrasuede paws, glass bead eyes, polyester stuffing. Photo by artist

Loris Hancock. Collection of Forest Dwellers, bears with fish: 4″ x 1¾″ x 1½″ (10.2 x 4.4 x 3.8 cm), bears on all 4 legs: 2¾″ x 3″ x 6″ (7 x 7.6 x 15.2 cm), bear with frog: 7″ x 3″ x 3″ (17.8 x 7.6 x 7.6 cm), 2000. Mohair, hand-painted Ultrasuede fish, beaded minibear fabric frog. Photo by artist

Donna Nielsen. Sebastian, 15″ (38.1 cm), 2000. Mohair/alpaca blend, Ultasuede paws, German glass eyes. Photo by artist

Kathy Rouhier. Ormsby, 16″ (40.6 cm), 1998. Vintage horsehair sleigh blanket. Photo by artist

Cherlynn Rose Cathro. Hershey, 4″ (10.2 cm), 1998. German long pile miniature fabric, Ultrasuede paws, onyx eyes, polyester and glass-bead stuffing. Photo by artist

Rotraud Ilisch. Two Honeybears, left: 12″ (30.5 cm), right: 2½″ (6.4 cm), 1995. Alpaca, mini plush. Photo by artist

Rosey Day. Taquin, 3⅛″ (8 cm), 2000. Cashmere minibear fabric, Ultrasuede, onyx beads. Photo by artist

Tami Eveslage. Cozy, 13″ x 11″ x 12″ (33 x 27.9 x 30.5 cm), 2000. Extra-dense mohair, Ultrasuede paws and mouth, pearl cotton embroidered nose, glass eyes, polyester and pellet stuffing. Photo by artist

Cherlynn Rose Cathro.
Samuel, 24˝ (61 cm),
1997. Featherfluff
mohair, blown-glass eyes,
internal growler, polyester
and cinnamon-scented
plastic-pellet stuffing.
Photo by artist

Beth Hill. Junior Jones,
21˝ (53.34 cm), 2000.
Mohair, Ultrasuede,
glass eyes, polyester and
pellet stuffing.
Photo by Haywood Hill

Edie Barlishen. Leaving Home, top: 5˝ (12.7 cm), bottom: 2˝
(5.1 cm), 1999. Upholstery velvet, Ultrasuede paws, glass
bead eyes, polyester stuffing, resin suitcase. Photo by artist

Beth Hill. Bad Hair Boys, 12˝ (30.5 cm), 2000. Mohair,
Ultrasuede, glass eyes, polyester stuffing. Photo by Haywood Hill

Carol-Lynn Rössel Waugh. 9 Bears, from 2˝ (5.1 cm) to 28˝ (71.1
cm), 1995. German distressed mohair, cotton velveteen paws, glass
eyes, plastic-pellet stuffing. Photo by artist

Pam Washburn. Digger, 7″ x 2½″ x 1½″ (17.8 x 6.4 x 3.2 cm), 1999. German mohair, glass eyes, polyester stuffing. Photo by Haywood Hill

Cherlynn Rose Cathro. Tommy, 4″ (10.2 cm), 1998. Cashmere, onyx eyes, polyester and glass-bead stuffing. Photo by artist.

The Boyd Collection Limited®. Webber Vanguard, 16″ (40.6 cm), 1999. Bean stuffing. Photo by Simone & Associates

The Boyd Collection Limited®. Bamboo Bearington, 14″ (35.6 cm), 2000. Mohair, custom-dyed fur, leather paws, silk jacquard neckbow. Photo by Simone & Associates

Kaylee Nilan. Mother and Cubs, mother: 42″ (106.7 cm), cubs: 24″ (61 cm), 1998. French plush, hand-made resin mouth, nose and claws, glass eyes. Photo by Mark Lafond

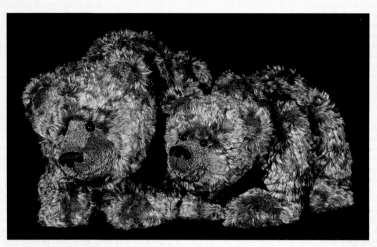

Marcia Sibol. Noella Bella, 12″ (30.5 cm), 2000.
Curly matted mohair, shoe button eyes, polyester
and pellet stuffing, vintage lace collar. Photo by
Hill Signature Portraits

Beth Hill. Mama and Baby Silvertip, left: 10″ x 19″ (25.4 x 48.3 cm), right:
7″ x 13½″ (17.8 x 34.3 cm), 2000. Mohair, Ultrasuede paws, glass eyes,
internal growler, polyester stuffing. Photo by Haywood Hill

Carol-Lynn Rössel Waugh. Mascot and Maria, left: 18″ (45.7
cm), right: 14″ (35.6 cm), 1995. German mohair, cotton
velveteen paws, glass eyes. Photo by artist

Monty and Joe Sours. Big John, 28″ (71.1 cm), 2000.
Mohair (the artists sheared the goat themselves!).
Photo by Joe Sours

Russ. Radcliffe™, left: 6″ (15.2 cm), middle: 17″ (43.2 cm), right: 13″ (33 cm), 1994. Plush. Photo by Russ Berrie & Co, Inc.

Heike Boam. Mother and Cub, left: 3″ (7.6 cm), right: 4″ (10.2 cm), 2000. Cotton viscose, hand-painted face and paws, varnished nose and lips, embroidered teeth. Photo by artist

Ulli Bowman. Grizzo & Ping & Pong, dinosaur: 8⅛″ x 4″ x 10¹/₁₆″ (21.5 x 10 x 26 cm), bears: 2″ (5 cm), 2000. Premium plush, curly German mohair, German mohair, cashmere miniature fabric, fish skin, feathers, antique beads, pearls, glass eyes, bead eyes, silk paper, leather, cork for base. Photo by artist

Cherlynn Rose Cathro. Bernard, 6½″ (16.5 cm), 1996. German synthetic with guard hairs, Ultrasuede paws, onyx eyes, polyester and steel-shot stuffing. Photo by artist

Edie Barlishen. Good Neighbours, 13″ x 13½″ (33 x 34.3 cm), 1996. Mohair, Ultrasuede paws, glass eyes, polyester, steel- and plastic-pellet stuffing. Photo by artist

Mindi Koudelka. Toffee, 3″ x 1″ x 1″ (7.6 x 2.5 x 2.5 cm), 2000. Cashmere upholstery fabric, pearl cotton nose, onyx eyes. Photo by artist

Vicky Lougher. Timothy, 7″ x 3″ x 2″ (17.8 x 7.6 x 5.1 cm), 1998. Mohair. Photo by artist

Denise Purrington. Tofu, 14″ (35.6 cm), 2000. Tea-dyed string mohair, wool felt paws, glass eyes. Photo by artist

Russ. Cosgrove™, 14″ (35.6 cm), 1998. Swirled plush, corduroy paws, satin ribbon. Photo by Russ Berrie & Co, Inc.

The Boyd Collection Limited. Alabaster B. Bigfoot, 18″ (45.7 cm), 2000. Bean stuffing, silk neckbow. Photo by Simone & Associates

Russ. Pennington, 19″ (48.3 cm), 1999. High pile plush, organza ribbon. Photo by Russ Berrie & Co, Inc.

Janet Desjardine. Woodsprite, 3″ (7.6 cm), 1998. Upholstery fabric, Ultrasuede. Photo by Wayne Desjardine

Kaylee Nilan. Snowshoe Bear, 24″ (61 cm), 1991. French plush, hand-made resin mouth, nose and claws, glass eyes. Photo by Don Brannon

Russ. Wesley, 10″ (25.4 cm), 2000. Two-tone tip-dyed plush. Photo by Russ Berrie & Co, Inc.

Ginger T. Brame. Beck, 6″ x 3″ x 2″ (15 x 7.6 x 5.1 cm), 2000. Mohair, suede, pearl cotton, glass beads, glass eyes, polyester stuffing. Photo by artist

Carol-Lynn Rössel Waugh. Mini Maria, 2″ (5.1 cm), 1994.
Distressed German mohair.
Photo by artist

Jean and Jan Olsen. Big Ben, 48″ (122 cm), 2000. Mohair,
Ultrasuede paws, glass eyes. Photo by Bob O'Brion

Shelly Haugen. Bhimsha, 18″ (45.7 cm),
2000. Tipped mohair, hand-sculpted
polymer clay face. Photo by artist

Monty and Joe Sours. Otto, 15″
(38.1 cm), 1999. Hand-distressed alpaca (the artists
sheared the llama themselves!).
Photo by Joe Sours

Monty and Joe Sours. Jackie, 12″
(30.5 cm), 1993. Mohair (the artists
sheared the goat themselves!). Photo
by Joe Sours

Jean and Jan Olsen. Logan, 18˝ (45.7 cm), 1999. German mohair, Ultrasuede paws, hand-made glass eyes. Photo by Bob O'Brion

Jean and Jan Olsen. Lacy, 14˝ (35.6 cm), 2000. German mohair, Ultrasuede paws, hand-made glass eyes. Photo by Bob O'Brion

Jean and Jan Olsen. RIO, 24˝ (61 cm), 1998. German mohair, Ultrasuede paws, glass eyes. Photo by Bob O'Brion

Pat Murphy. Brady, 16˝ (40.6 cm), 2000. Hand-dyed mohair, darkened ears and muzzle. Photo by artist

Deborah Stewart. Foster, 18˝ (45.7 cm), 1997. German plush, pellet and polyester stuffing. Photo by artist

Monty and Joe Sours. 4 Pandas, left: 12″ (30.5 cm), middle left: 10″ (25.4 cm), middle right: 17″ (43.2 cm), right: 28″ (71.1 cm), 1999. Mohair (the artists sheared the goat themselves!). Photo by Joe Sours

Bette Carter. McDougle, 18″ (45.7 cm), 1997. Distressed mohair, double wool felt paws, shoe button eyes, excelsior and polyester stuffing. Photo by artist

Mary Daub. Father Bear, 65″ x 24″ x 24″ (165.1 x 61 x 61 cm), 2000. Imported synthetic fur, leather, glass taxidermy eyes, wood base. Photo by John Mulliken

Robert Bergsmann. Rufus A. Hembold, 17″ x 7″ x 6″ (43.2 x 17.8 x 15.2 cm), 1999. German alpaca, mohair, suede leather, glass eyes, internal growler, polyester stuffing. Photo by artist

Shelly Haugen. Kalden, 18″ (45.7 cm), 2000. Extra-dense English mohair, hand-sculpted polymer clay face. Photo by artist

Monty and Joe Sours. Gnarley and Gnarley Jr., *left: 21˝ (53.34 cm), right: 15˝ (38.1 cm), 1987 and 1988. Mohair (the artists sheared the goat themselves!). Photo by Joe Sours*

Deborah Stewart. Tattered Treasure, *7˝ (17.8 cm), 1998. Mohair, wool felt, excelsior. Photo by artist*

Brigit Charles. Giggles, *8˝ (20.3 cm), 2000. Left: mohair, right: woven synthetic fur, suede paws, minibear fabric mouths. Photo by Christina MacDonald*

Blanche Blakeny. Arlecchino, *15˝ x 7˝ x 5˝ (38.1 x 17.8 x 12.7 cm), 2000. Matted mohair, glass eyes, hand-made Ultrasuede hats. Photo by artist*

Sherri Creamer. Bud, *22˝ x 8˝ x 6˝ (55.9 x 20.3 x 15.2 cm), 2000. Recycled mink, leather paws, German glass eyes, polyester stuffing. Photo by artist*

Kathleen Wallace. Fletcher, 22″ (55.9 cm), 1998. Sparse mohair, antiqued and distressed. Photo by artist

Lisa Applebeary. Lollipop, 5½″ (14 cm), 2000. Mohair, German plush, hand-stitched nose, glass eyes, sheer ribbon. Photo by artist

Sherri Creamer. Sebastian, 19″ x 10″ x 8″ (48.3 x 25.4 x 20.3 cm), 2000. Recycled mink, leather paws, glass eyes, polyester stuffing. Photo by artist

Sheila Yates-Vuu. Hugs, 3½″ x 1½″ x 1″ (8.9 x 3.8 x 2.5 cm), 2000. Upholstery cashmere, quilt-thread nose, onyx eyes, quilt batting stuffing. Photo by artist

Mary Daub. Baby Bear, 32″ x 12″ x 12″ (81.2 x 30.5 x 30.5 cm), 2000. Imported synthetic fur, leather quilted paws, leather mouth, sculpted rubber nose, airbrushed face, taxidermy eyes. Photo by John Mulliken

Sheila Yates-Vuu. Gumdrop, 3½″ x 1½″ x 1″ (8.9 x 3.8 x 2.5 cm), 2000. Upholstery velvet, button-thread nose, onyx eyes, quilt batting stuffing, silk organza ribbon. Photo by artist

Sue Ann Holcomb. Butterscotch, 20″ (50.8 cm), 2000. German and English mohair, Ultrasuede paws, excelsior, steel-shot, plastic-pellet, and polyester stuffing. Photo by artist

Pat Harmon. Mary Ann, 13″ (33 cm), 2000. Recycled mink, Ultrasuede paws, embroidered nose and mouth, glass eyes. Photo by artist

Martha DeRaimo-Burch. Teddy R., 15″ (38.1 cm), 1999. Mohair. Photo by artist

Pat Lyons. Edelweiss, 9½″ x 4½″ x 2½″ (24.1 x 11.4 x 6.4 cm), 2000. Bone-feathered mohair, Ultrasuede paws, German blown-glass eyes, curly mohair hat and neckband. Photo by artist

Riëtte Steenkamp. Pierette Signature, 16″ x 6″ x 3½″ (40.6 x 15.2 x 8.9 cm), 1997. German mohair, Ultrasuede paws, glass eyes, polyester and pellet stuffing. Photo by artist

Bette Carter. Fitz William, 13″ (33 cm), 1999. Hand-distressed mohair, Rexine (antique) fabric paws, antique shoe button eyes. Photo by artist

Bette Carter. Benjamin, Patrick, and Edward, 18″ (45.7 cm), 1998. Mohair, Rexine (antique) fabric paws, antique shoe button eyes, internal German growler. Photo by artist

Mary Ann Gebhardt. Lemon Fairy, 1¾″ (4.4 cm), 2000. Cashmere, Ultrasuede paws, glass bead eyes. Photo by Tom Sanchirico

Michele Talbot. Cow Bell, 3.5″ (8.9 cm), 1999. Upholstery fabric, Ultrasuede paws, polyester stuffing. Photo by artist

Chris Winebrenner. Emerson, 22″ x 10″ x 10″ (55.9 x 25.4 x 25.4 cm), 1998. Mohair, Ultrasuede paws, polymer clay teeth, polyester and glass-bead stuffing. Photo by artist

Hifumi I. Adams. Chuckle, 15″ x 4″ x 3″ (38.1 x 10.2 x 7.6 cm), 2000. Mohair, hand-painted face, ears, and paws, antique shoe button eyes, polyester and steel-shot stuffing. Photo by artist

Michele Talbot. Kandy Kane, 7″ (17.8 cm), 1999. Mohair, metallic-thread nose, polyester and glass-bead stuffing, candy cane button. Photo by artist

Hifumi I. Adams. Wade Bear, 5″ x 2½″ x 2″ (12.7 x 6.4 x 5.1 cm), 2000. Distressed mohair, virgin wool paws, German glass eyes. Photo by artist

Pamela Wooley. Bellamy, 13″ (33 cm), 1999. English mohair. Photo by artist

Jackie Strecker. Wendell: A Tired Clown, 17″ x 9″ x 7″ (43.2 x 22.9 x 17.8 cm), 1999. Mohair. Photo by Bob Strecker

Jackie Strecker. Old Saint Nick, 18″ x 19″ x 7″ (45.7 x 48.3 x 17.8 cm), 1998. Mohair, hand-woven outfit and trim. Photo by Bob Strecker.

Riëtte Steenkamp. Charlie the Chef, 15″ x 4″ x 3″ (38.1 x 10.2 x 7.6 cm), 1999. German mohair, Ultrasuede paws, glass eyes, polyester and pellet stuffing. Photo by artist

Pamela Wooley. Williams, 21″ (53.34 cm), 2000. Curly German mohair, suede paws, waxed nose, antique sleigh bell. Photo by artist

Kathy S. Kluges. Baby, 18″ x 7½″ x 8″ (45.7 x 19.1 x 20.3 cm), 1997. Mohair, Ultrasuede, polyester and plastic-pellet stuffing. Photo by Olan Mills

Kathy S. Kluges. Bear, 22″ x 33″ (55.9 x 83.8 cm), 1998. Mohair, Ultrasuede, German glass eyes, polyester and plastic-pellet stuffing. Photo by Olan Mills

Donna Nielsen. Riley, 31″ (78.7 cm), 2000. Mohair, appliquéd paws, hand-dyed muzzle, German glass eyes, polyester and plastic-pellet filling. Photo by artist

Carol-Lynn Rössel Waugh. Nicholas Carl Jonathan Björn, 18″ (45.7 cm), 1995. German distressed mohair, cotton velveteen paws, glass eyes. Photo by artist

Pilar Friesen. Bud and Bud Jr., top: 12˝ (30.5 cm), bottom: 8˝ (20.3 cm), 1999. Mohair, suede paws, glass eyes, pellet, steel-shot, and cotton stuffing, suede hats, wired ribbon. Photo by artist

Janet Reeves. Lorelei, 20˝ (50.8 cm). Mohair, Ultasuede paws, glass eyes. Photo by artist

Joel Hoy. Joseph, 22˝ (55.9 cm), 1999. Curly mohair, wool felt paws, glass eyes, polyester stuffing, pieced coat. Photo by artist

Connie Hindmarsh. Avery Byard and Gracie the Puppy, 12˝ (30.5 cm), 2000. Mohair. Photo by artist

Olivia Russel. Clancy, 22″ (55.9 cm), 1999. Mohair, leather, faux fur. Photo by John Russell

Janet Reeves. Brianna, 20″ (50.8 cm); Over-dyed mohair, Ultrasuede paws, glass eyes. Photo by artist

Bonnie Bergman. Bear in Love, 11″ (27.9 cm), 1999. Recycled beaver felt hat, cinnamon heart. Photo by Jeff Bayne

Carol-Lynn Rössel Waugh. Hand Painted Bears, 15″ (38.1 cm), 1996. Hand-painted German mohair, cotton velveteen paws, glass eyes. Photo by artist

Left: Cherlynn Rose Cathro. The Caroler, 7½″ (19.1 cm), 1999. Cashmere, embroidery floss, onyx bead eyes, polyester, glass-beads and steel-shot stuffing. Photo by artist

Right: Kathy Rouhier. Jarod & Arthur, 21″ (53.34 cm) and 12″ (30.5 cm), 1996. Created from the owner's childhood blanket. Photo by artist

Anita Ekelo. Bug, Buzz, Butt: Let's Celebrate Springtime!, 2¾″ x 3¹⁵⁄₁₆″ x 1³⁄₁₆″ (7 x 10 x 3 cm), 1999. Short pile upholstery, glass bead eyes, cotton, tule. Photo by artist

Jackie Ryan. Gone Surfing, 13½″ x 9″ x 11½″ (34.3 x 22.9 x 29.2 cm), 2000. Mohair, Ultrasuede paws, glass eyes, polyester and steel-shot stuffing. Photo by P. Ryan

Olivia Russel. SnowBelle: A Polar Bear & Her Pet Seal, *12˝ (30.5 cm), 2000. Alpaca, suede, appliqué paws. Photo by John Russell*

Kathlyn Gordon. Spring Impressions, *7˝ (17.8 cm), 2000. Hand-dyed German mohair, Ultrasuede paws, onyx eyes, polyester and glass-pellet stuffing, silk and organdy ribbon. Photo by artist*

Nancy L. Bax. Miss Cherry Chocolate, *3½˝ x 1½˝ x 1½˝ (8.9 x 3.8 x 3.8 cm), 1998. Upholstery velvet, onyx eyes, polyester stuffing. Photo by artist*

Sue and Randall Foskey. Black Bears, *from left to right: 12˝ (30.5 cm), 14˝ (34.3 cm), 16˝ (40.6 cm), 18˝ (45.7 cm), 1996. Mohair, felt silk-screened paws, glass eyes, polyester and pellet stuffing, suede bell collars. Photo by Randall Foskey*

Kathlyn Gordon. Kathlyn's Colorful Creations, 7″ to 8″ (17.8 to 20.3 cm), 2000. Hand-dyed German mohair, Ultrasuede paws, onyx eyes, polyester and glass-pellet stuffing, silk or organdy bows. Photo by artist

Kathlyn Gordon. Sugarbritches, 7″ (17.8 cm), 2000. German mohair, imitation leather paws, onyx eyes, polyester and glass-pellet stuffing, silk ribbon with a teddy bear charm. Photo by artist

Kathy Rouhier. Smudge, 17″ (43.2 cm), 2000. Vintage mohair sleigh blanket. Photo by artist

Kathy Rouhier. Cocoa, 17″ (43.2 cm), 2000. Vintage mohair sleigh blanket. Photo by artist

Debra LuBien. Basil, 14″ (35.6 cm), 2000. Mohair, Ultrasuede. Photo by artist

Carol Martin. Shorty, 24″ (61 cm), 1999. Mohair. Photo by Alice French

Janet Changfoot. Shaun, 22″ (55.9 cm), 2000. Mohair, appliquéd suede toes. Photo by artist

Ingrid Smith. Ragamuffin, 15⅜″ x 8″ x 6″ (39 x 20 x 15 cm), 2000. Sparse mohair, glass eyes, wool stuffing. Photo by artist

Kaylee Nilan. Brown Bear Family, right: 36″ (91.44 cm), left: 40″ (101.6 cm), cubs: 24″ (61 cm), 1994. French plush, hand-made resin mouth, nose and claws, glass eyes. Photo by Mark Lafond

Ingrid Smith. Lumber Bear, 16″ x 9½″ x 6″ (40 x 24 x 15 cm), 1999. Mohair, felt paws, glass eyes, wool stuffing. Photo by artist

Ginger Heimbuch. Button, Teddy's Bear, 13″ x 6″ x 4¾″ (33 x 15.2 x 12.1 cm), 2000. German mohair, Ultrasuede paws, hand-embroidered nose and mouth, German shoe button eyes, old-style German tilt growler, polyester, pellet and excelsior stuffing. Photo by artist

Ginger Heimbuch. Everett Bärle, 17″ x 8½″ x 7¾″ (43.2 x 21.6 x 19.7 cm), 2000. English dense and wavy mohair, Ultrasuede paws, embroidered nose and mouth, vintage shoe button eyes, old-style German tilt growler, polyester, pellet, and excelsior stuffing. Photo by artist

Ginger Heimbuch. Rufuss Teddybär, 14″ x 6½″ x 6″ (35.6 x 16.5 x 15.2 cm), 2000. German mohair, German mohair paws, German shoe button eyes, German glass nose, embroidered mouth and eyebrows, twine necklace of old buttons. Photo by artist

Jenny Walton. Bronwyn, 6″ x 9″ (15.2 x 22.9 cm), 1999. German mohair, buzzard eyes, polyester and glass-bead stuffing, hand-dyed vintage lace. Photo by Peter Laverick

Becky Gray. Bear Whistles, 4″ x 3″ x 3″ (10.2 x 7.6 x 7.6 cm), 2000. Raku fired clay. Photo by Sandra Stambaugh

Victorya Blue Lightning Snake. Dulé, 3″ (7.6 cm), 2000. Cashmere suede, Ultrasuede paws, glass bead eyes. Photo by Sandra Stambaugh

Russ. Sir Ellwood™, 17″ (43.2 cm), 1999. Vintage plush, suede paws. Photo by Russ Berrie & Co, Inc.

Victorya Blue Lightning Snake. Bee Butt Bear, 15″ (38.1 cm), 1998. Hand-dyed German plush, Ultrasuede paws and muzzle, German glass eyes. Photo by Sandra Stambaugh

"Dar" Malinowski. Billy Bear, 22″ x 13″ x 7″ (55.9 x 33 x 17.8 cm), 2000. Mohair, sculptured felt face, glass eyes, internal growler, kapok-excelsior stuffing. Photo by Michael Malinowski

Beverly White. "Drawing The Line…" T.R. And the Berryman Bear, left: 30″ (76.2 cm), right: 23″ (58.4 cm), 1998. Mohair, leather paws, glass eyes, head growler. Photo by artist

"Dar" Malinowski. Red Bear, 14″ x 7″ x 5″ (35.6 x 17.8 x 12.7 cm), 1999. Old wool coat, velvet nose, glass eyes, kapok-excelsior stuffing. Photo by Michael Malinowski

Beverly White. The Happy Tymes Gang, *from 18″ (45.7 cm) to 30″ (76.2 cm), 1995. Mohair, leather, glass eyes, internal growlers, polyester-pellet stuffing. Photo by artist*

Rosey Day. Anton, Fruit Tingle, *and* Williken, *left: 3″ (7.7 cm), middle: 3¼″, right: 2½″ (6.5 cm). Vintage long-file upholstery velvet, cashmere, shiny upholstery velvet, ultrasuede paws, onyx eyes, hand-shaded faces. Photo by artist*

Brigit Charles. Arctic Thule, *8½″ x 16″ (21.6 x 40.6 cm), 1999. Mohair, leather nose, glass eyes. Photo by Lyn Syme*

Dee Dee Triplett. Nuisance Bear Dancing Under the Laughing Moon *and* Nuisance Bear Coming Over You Like a Clear Blue Puffy-White-Cloud Day, Wafting By on the Breeze...Snatching an Apple on the Way, *20″ x 13″ x 8″ (50.8 x 33 x 20.3 cm), 1999. Suedecloth, wire, stone, paint. Photo by Robert Triplett*

Kaylee Nilan. Niels and Katje, 31″ (78.7 cm), 1994. French plush, hand-made resin mouth, nose and claws, glass eyes, wool clothing. Photo by Mark Lafond

Carol-Lynn Rössel Waugh. Geoffrey, 24″ (61 cm), 1993. German woven synthetic plush. Photo by artist

Carol-Lynn Rössel Waugh. Three Bears, left: 16″ (40.6 cm), middle: 14½″ (36.8 cm), right: 7½″ (19.1 cm), 1995. German distressed mohair, plastic-pellet stuffing. Photo by artist

Carol-Lynn Rössel Waugh. 2 Bears Studying Swedish, 18″ (45.7 cm), 1995. German distressed mohair, cotton velveteen paws, glass eyes. Photo by artist

Master Pattern: Teddy Bear # 1

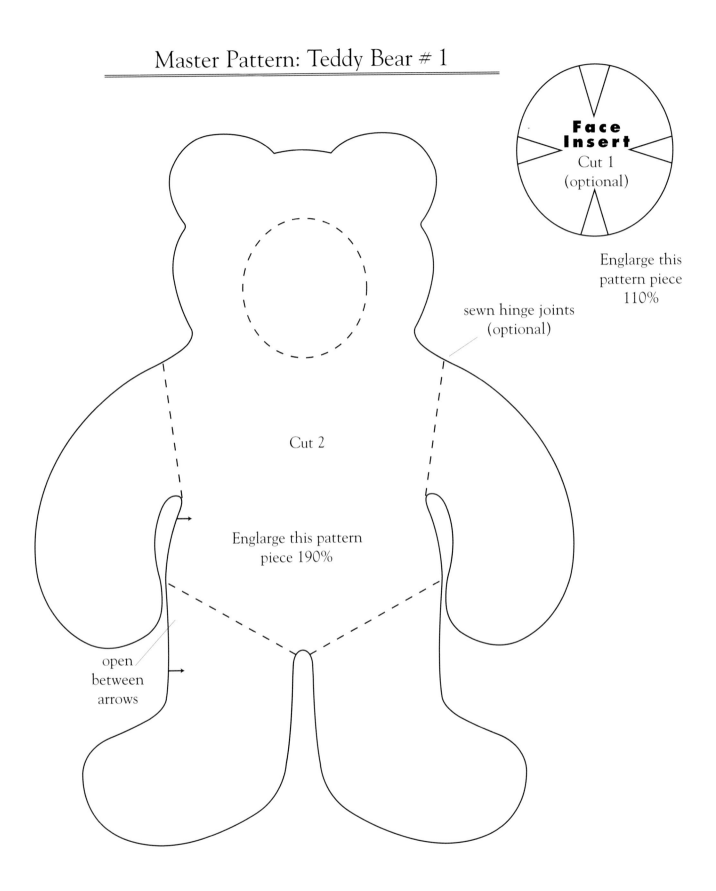

Face Insert
Cut 1
(optional)

Englarge this
pattern piece
110%

sewn hinge joints
(optional)

Cut 2

Englarge this pattern
piece 190%

open
between
arrows

Master Pattern: Teddy Bear # 2

Englarge all pattern pieces 200%

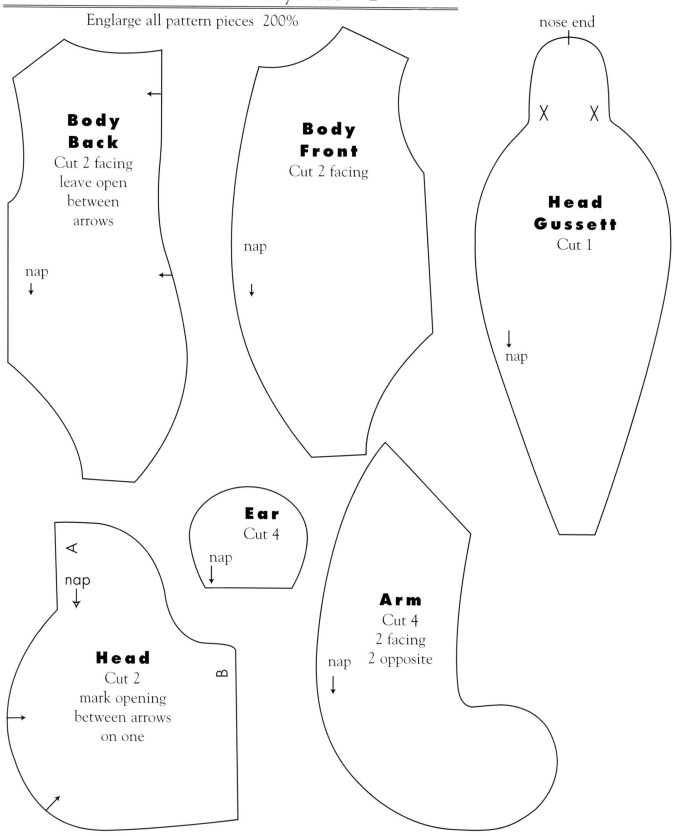

Body Back
Cut 2 facing
leave open
between
arrows

nap

Body Front
Cut 2 facing

nap

nose end

Head Gussett
Cut 1

nap

Ear
Cut 4

nap

A

nap

B

Head
Cut 2
mark opening
between arrows
on one

Arm
Cut 4
2 facing
2 opposite

nap

Bear #2 continues on page 134.

Teddy Bear # 2 (continued from page 133)   # Master Pattern: Teddy Bear # 3

Englarge all pattern pieces 200%

Englarge all pattern pieces 200%

nose end

nose end

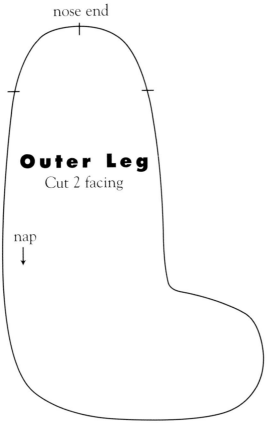

Outer Leg
Cut 2 facing

nap
↓

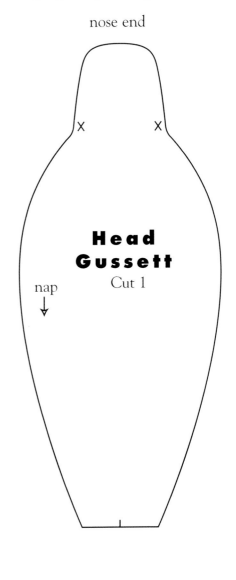

Head Gussett
Cut 1

nap
↓

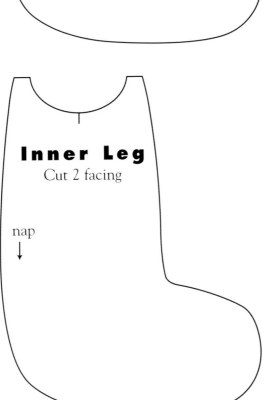

Inner Leg
Cut 2 facing

nap
↓

Teddy Bear # 3 (continued from page 134)

Englarge all pattern pieces 200%

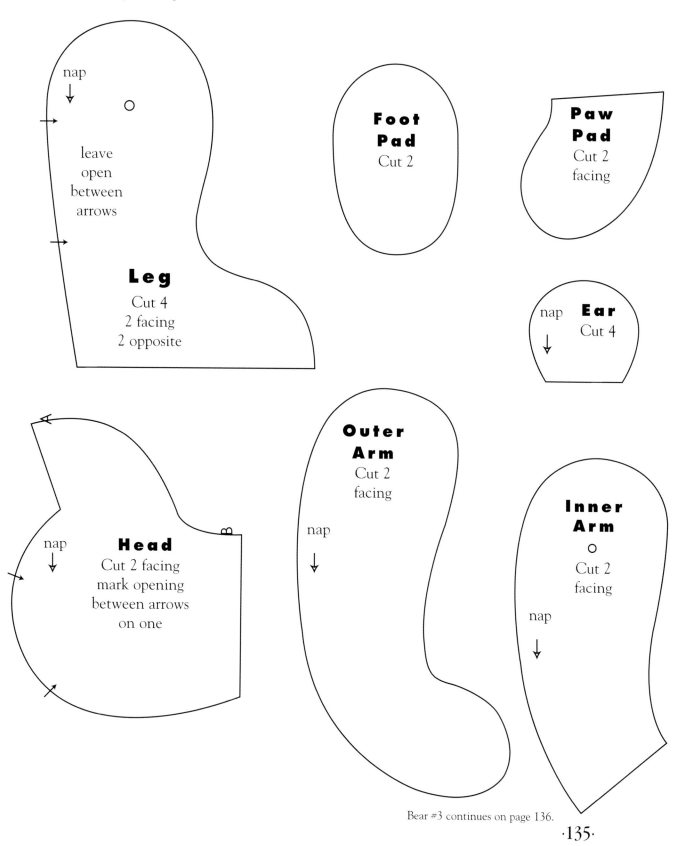

Leg
Cut 4
2 facing
2 opposite

nap

leave open between arrows

Foot Pad
Cut 2

Paw Pad
Cut 2 facing

nap **Ear**
Cut 4

Head
Cut 2 facing
mark opening
between arrows
on one

nap

Outer Arm
Cut 2
facing

nap

Inner Arm
Cut 2
facing

nap

Bear #3 continues on page 136.

Teddy Bear # 3 (continued from page 135)

Englarge all pattern pieces 200%

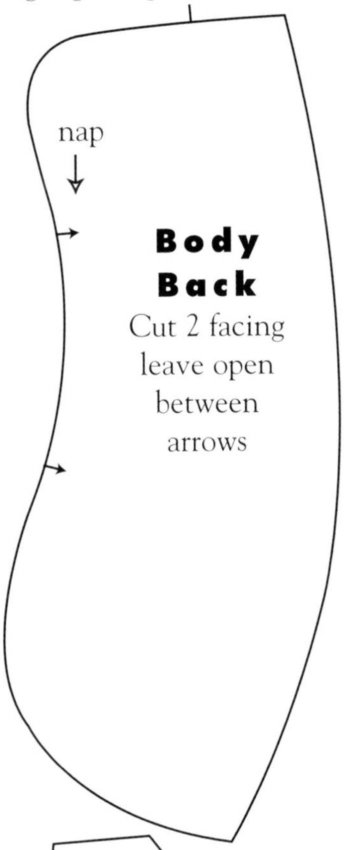
nap
Body
Back
Cut 2 facing
leave open
between
arrows

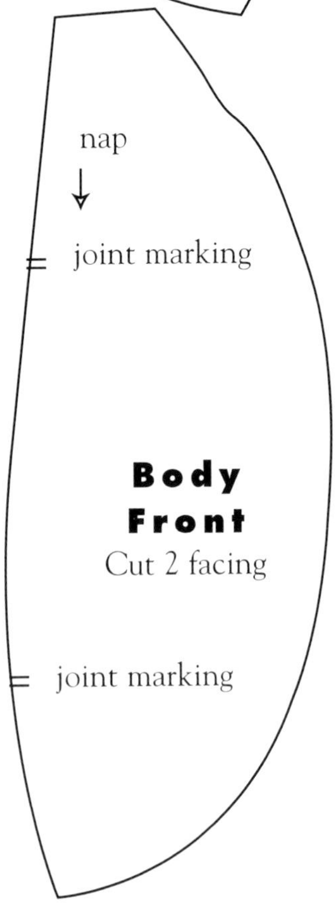
nap
joint marking
Body
Front
Cut 2 facing
joint marking

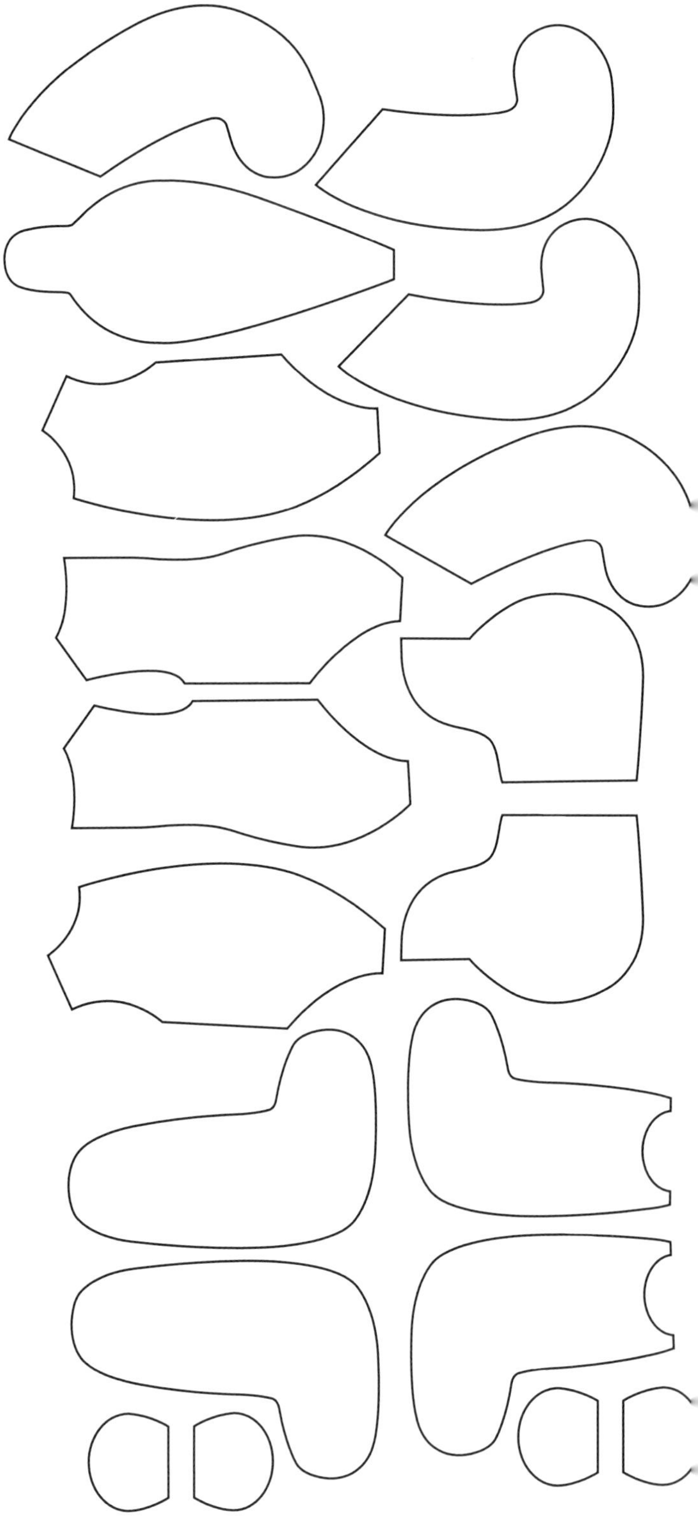

Autumn Ted

Pattern pieces are actual size

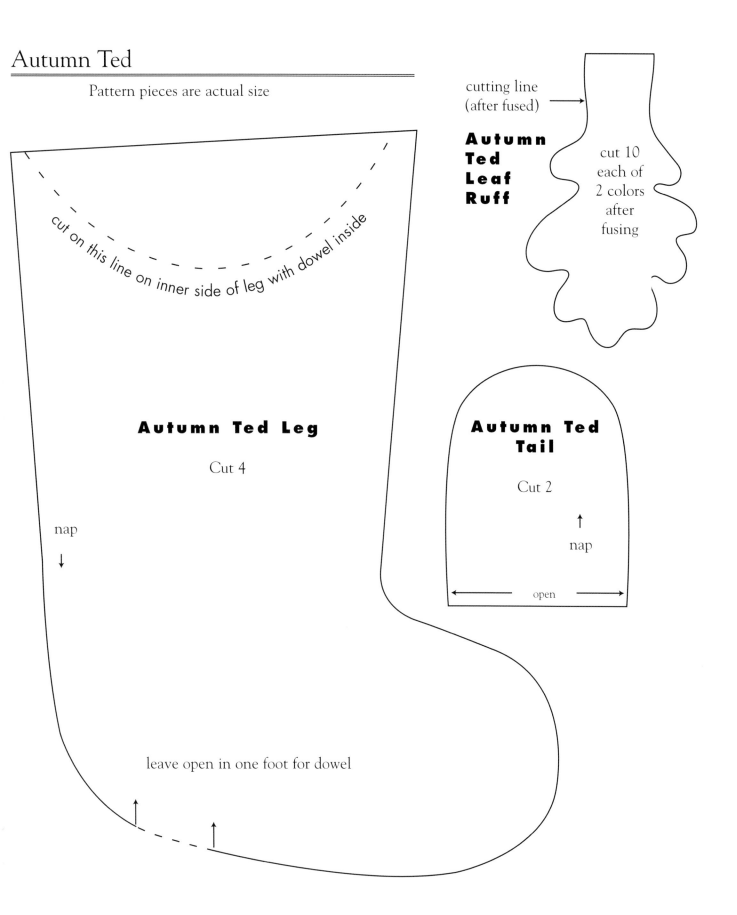

cutting line
(after fused)

**Autumn
Ted
Leaf
Ruff**

cut 10
each of
2 colors
after
fusing

cut on this line on inner side of leg with dowel inside

Autumn Ted Leg

Cut 4

nap
↓

**Autumn Ted
Tail**

Cut 2

↑
nap

open

leave open in one foot for dowel

Merry Prankster Harlequin Bear

Englarge all pattern pieces 170%

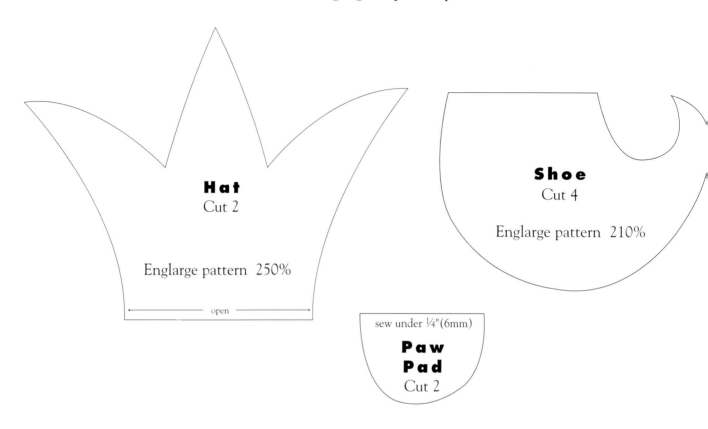

Hat
Cut 2

Englarge pattern 250%

open

Shoe
Cut 4

Englarge pattern 210%

sew under ¼"(6mm)

Paw Pad
Cut 2

Theodore E. Bear

Pattern piece is actual size

Leaf Patch

Aromatherapy Bear

Pattern pieces are actual size

Tie-On Heart
Cut 2 per heart

Inner Ear
Cut 2

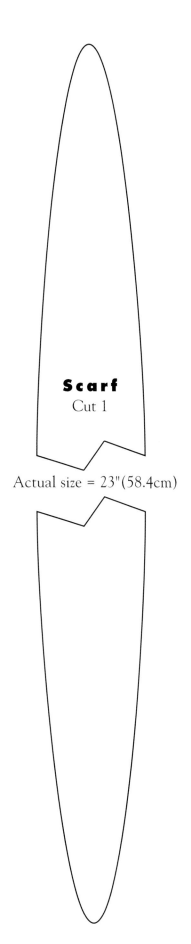

Scarf
Cut 1

Actual size = 23"(58.4cm)

Matilda's Great Escape

Englarge all pattern pieces 330%

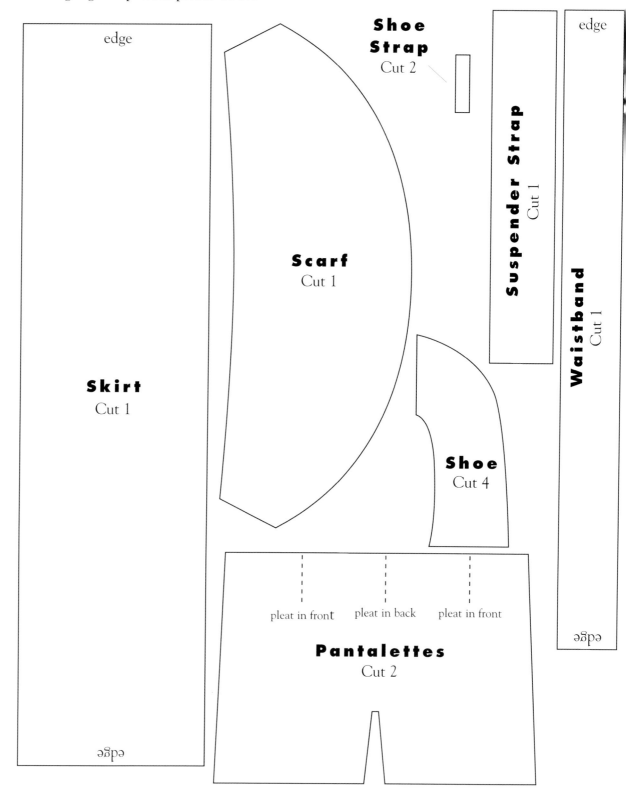

edge

Shoe Strap
Cut 2

edge

Suspender Strap
Cut 1

Waistband
Cut 1

Scarf
Cut 1

Skirt
Cut 1

Shoe
Cut 4

edge

pleat in front   pleat in back   pleat in front

Pantalettes
Cut 2

edge

edge

CONTRIBUTORS

Pattern Designer and Book Consultant

BETH HILL has been doing crafts of all sorts for most of her life and has been designing, sewing, and selling teddy bears through her business, Bethbears, for 12 years.

She received her first teddy bear at age two and a small rabbit shortly thereafter. The bear, known as "T.K." for "Teddy Cuddles," and the rabbit, "Petie," were her constant companions throughout her childhood. Sitting on a little stool near her grandmother's sewing machine, she began learning how to make clothes for T.K. and Petie as soon as she was old enough to hold a needle. She also developed a lasting love of sewing. When she discovered that patterns existed for teddy bears, there was no stopping her. She worked with various patterns and books to develop her own style of jointed, mohair bears in the spirit of the Steiff bears she had always wanted to own.

Beth says watching her teddy bears evolve from fabric to bear—and having them tell her a bit about their personalities as they come to life—is a great delight. "The process really takes me back to that fantasy land of childhood, which I would never want to lose touch with."

Teddy Bear Designers

VICTORYA BLUE LIGHTNING SNAKE has always pursued creative expression as a means of relaxation and meditation. She began with cold glass, then experimented with hot glass, then lampworking glass and beading. Since she collects dolls from India and *loves* fabric, she became interested several years ago in creating cloth dolls and animals. She now collects myths and stories from indigenous peoples and translates them into one-of-a-kind dolls and animals.

BARBARA BUSSOLARI is a retired Massachusetts schoolteacher now living in the mountains of western North Carolina. For the past 20 years, she has designed, made, and sold cards using handmade and hand-decorated papers and handwoven material. She is now exploring and expanding into paper jewelry and dolls made with handwoven materials and handmade papers.

MARY STANLEY CASADONTE enjoys life—and for 30 years has been sewing anything she can get her hands on.

ELAINE MCPHERSON is a designer of novelty items, including bears, and has created her own line of "Toots," which includes 20 different animals. She is also an artist, poet, and tailor.

TERRY TAYLOR is a multitalented artist whose work ranges from beading and lamp making to gilding and the pique-assiette mosaic technique. He allows bits and pieces of many art forms to influence his one-of-a-kind creations.

KIM TIBBALS-THOMPSON lives in Waynesville, North Carolina. She is a frequent contributor to craft books and enjoys drawing, sewing, gardening, herbal crafting, and broom making. By day, she is a graphic designer.

DEE DEE TRIPLETT has designed and taught fiber art for more than 25 years. She finds creating freelance designs for various publications a great excuse for collecting more fabric scraps and other fun stuff. Attention to color, detail, and a sense of movement and whimsical elegance are all important parts of her work and contribute to her desire to elicit positive, joyful responses in a too-often negative world. She considers it a privilege that her "work" is dancing with cloth and playing with rainbows of color.

TRICIA TUSA has been writing and illustrating children's books for the last 18 years, and loves sculpting and sewing the characters she draws for her books. She also works as a freelance artist.

A love of both history and the arts has been a key note in the life of YVONNE WILLIAMS, so it made sense to translate these interests and talents into her own business: Perqs, specializing in gifts and collectibles. Along with partner Eleanor Williams (who is also Yvonne's redheaded mother), Yvonne enjoys designing with classically elegant fabrics, such as silk, velvet, and brocade, adding her own flair for sparkle and color. Perqs' current focus is a line of porcelain dolls in vintage-style costumes. For more information on the teddy bear she created for this book, visit her website at www.perqs-plaza.com.

Continued on page 142

CONTRIBUTORS

Gallery Artists

HIFUMI I. ADAMS, 123 Wade Bears, Beaufort, South Carolina, USA

LISA APPLEBEARY, Applebeary Originals, Mission Viejo, California, USA

EDIE BARLISHEN, Bears by Edie, Alberta, Alberta, Canada

NANCY L. BAX, Nan's Bear Hug, London, Ontario, Canada

BONNIE BERGMAN, Mason, Wisconsin, USA

ROBERT BERGSMANN, Bergy Bears, Alameda, California, USA

BLANCHE BLAKENY, Blakeny Bears, Carlstadt, New Jersey, USA

VICTORYA BLUE LIGHTNING SNAKE, Q'ero Cantadora, Lake Toxaway, North Carolina, USA

HEIKE BOAM, Heike Boam & Bears, Staufen, Germany

ULLI BOWMAN, FetzerBear, Hornsby, New South Wales, Australia

GINGER T. BRAME, The Piece Parade, Raleigh, North Carolina, USA

BETTE CARTER, Trunk Bears, Salem, Oregon, USA

CHERLYNN ROSE CATHRO, Cherlynn Rose Handmade Collectibles, Cypress, Texas, USA

JANET CHANGFOOT, Changle Bears South Africa, Vincent, East London, South Africa

BRIGIT CHARLES, Brigit's Bears, Chidlow, Western Australia, Australia

SHERRI CREAMER, Alive Again Bears, Burbank, California, USA

MARY DAUB, Mary's Secret Garden, Stanton, Delaware, USA

ROSEY DAY, Hawthorne East, Victoria, Australia

MARTHA DERAIMO-BURCH, Martha's Bears, West Bend, Wisconsin, USA

JANET DESJARDINE, Tiny Teddies, Portage La Prarie, Manitoba, Canada

ANITA EKELO, AE Miniatures, Dordrecht, Netherlands

TAMI EVESLAGE, Bear It All, Cincinnati, Ohio, USA

MARY LOU FOLEY, Bayside Bears, Brewster, Massachusetts, USA

SUE AND RANDALL FOSKEY, Nostalgic Bears, Ocean View, Delaware, USA

PILAR FRIESEN, Teddies R' Friends, American Falls, Idaho, USA

MARY ANN GEBHARDT, Mary Ann Gebhardt Bears, Franklin Lakes, New Jersey, USA

KATHLYN GORDON, Bears by Kathlyn, Midland, Texas, USA

BECKY GRAY, Burnsville, North Carolina, USA

LORIS HANCOCK, Studio Seventy, Elanora, Queensland, Australia

PAT HARMON, Mama Bear, Unlimited, Belen, New Mexico, USA

SHELLY HAUGEN, Lizzie D TLC Bears, Alexander, North Dakota, USA

GINGER HEIMBUCH, The Bears of Tannenbaum Woods, Ferndale, California, USA

BETH HILL, BETHBEARS, Asheville, North Carolina, USA

CONNIE HINDMARSH, Connie Hindmarsh Studios, Norfolk, Virginia, USA

SUE ANN HOLCOMB, Past Time Bears, Double Oak, Texas, USA

JOEL HOY, Joel's Bears, Mission, Kansas, USA

ROTRAUD ILISCH, Bär & Co., Duelmen-Merfeld, Germany

KATHY S. KLUGES, KSK-Furever Yours, Dearborn, Michigan, USA

MINDI KOUDELKA, Tinybears.com, New Haven, Connecticut, USA

VICKY LOUGHER, Elegant Creations, Chesapeake, Virginia, USA

DEBRA LUBIEN, Mama LuBears, Valley Center, California, USA

PAT LYONS, Free Spirit Bears, Cottonwood, Arizona, USA

"DAR" MALINOWSKI, "Forever Yours," Linden, Michigan, USA

CAROL MARTIN, cmBEARS, Eureka Springs, Arizona, USA

GEORGINA MULLEY, Kingston, Queensland, Australia

PAT MURPHY, Murphy Bears, Ann Arbor, Michigan, USA

DONNA NIELSEN, Cookie's Critters, Bloomfield, New York, USA

KAYLEE NILAN, Beaver Valley, Kirkland, Washington, USA

JEAN and JAN OLSEN, Olsen Designs Inc., Rio, Wisconsin, USA

DENISE PURRINGTON, "Out of the Forest" Bears, Bellevue, Washington, USA

JANET REEVES, HUG-A-BEAR, Midland, Michigan, USA

KATHY ROUHIER, Thurston-McMindes Bears, Scotts Valley, California, USA

OLIVIA RUSSEL, Beary Jolly, Montrose, Victoria, Australia

JACKIE RYAN, Dragonslair Bears, Ilfracombe, North Devon, England, UK

MARCIA SIBOL, Bar Harbor Bears, Newark, Delaware, USA

INGRID SMITH, Ingrid Smith Filtmakerverksted, Geithus, Norway

RIËTTE STEENKAMP, Pierette Bears, Stellenbosch, South Africa

ACKNOWLEDGMENTS

DEBORAH STEWART, Stewart Studios, Acton, Massachuesetts USA

JACKIE STRECKER, Arbor, Vassar, Michigan, USA

MONTY and JOE SOURS, The Bear Lady, Golden City, Missouri, USA

MICHELE TALBOT, The Bear Cellar, Simi Valley, California, USA

DEE DEE TRIPLETT, Dee Dee Triplett, Inc., Bryson City, North Carolina, USA

KATHLEEN WALLACE, Stier Bears, Spring City, Pennsylvania, USA

JENNY WALTON, Prince Bishop Bears, Coxhoe, Durham, UK

PAM WASHBURN, Bears By P.A.W., Rutland, Vermont, USA

CAROL-LYNN RÖSSEL WAUGH, Winthrop, Maine, USA

BEVERLY WHITE, Happy Tymes Collectibles, DowningTown, Pennsylvania, USA

PAMELA WOOLEY, Pamela Wooley Collection, Laguna Niguel, California, USA

SHEILA YATES-VUU, Lincoln, Nebraska, USA

THE BOYD COLLECTION LIMITED®, Gettysburg, Pennsylvania, USA

RUSS, Oakland, New Jersey, USA

THE VERMONT TEDDY BEAR COMPANY®, Shelburne, Vermont, USA

As they say in the teddy bear world, a big bear hug to:

Ron Block and all the friendly folks at Edinburgh Imports, Inc., in Newbury Park, California, USA, who loaned us boxes full of wonderfully organized supplies and materials for our Bearmaking Basics photo shoot. For more information or to request a catalog, contact them at www.edinburgh.com or (805) 376-1700.

Those who entrusted us with their Best-Loved Bears in the World: Brian Caskey, Beth Hill, Marthe Le Van, Diana Light, Laure Snyder, Sandra Stambaugh, Terry Taylor, and Mary Thompson

The Teddy Bear Castle Museum, Nevada City, California, USA, for all of the vintage teddy bear postcards. Visit them at www.teddybearcastle.com.

The Theodore Roosevelt Collection, Harvard College Library, Cambridge, Massachusetts, USA, for the Clifford Berryman cartoon

All the suppliers of photographs of interesting, old, rare, and famous bears:

- Eden LLC, New York, New York, USA

- Anne Hofmann, Donnell Library Center, The New York Public Library, New York, New York, USA

- Eric M. Kluge of Gebr. BING Inc., Bamberg, Germany

- The Library of Congress, Washington, D.C., USA

- The Museum of Modern Art, Film Stills Archive, New York, New York, USA

- "Doc Pary" (Paralee Schluchtner), Arvada, Colorado, USA

- Yoshi Sekiguchi, Sun Arrow Co, Ltd., Tokyo, Japan, for photos from the Izu and Nasu Museums

- The Smithsonian Institution, Museum of American History, Washington, D.C., USA

- John and Judy Sparrow, The Bear Museum, Petersfield, Hampshire, UK

- Teddy-Hermann GmbH, Hirschaid, Germany

- The U.S. Forest Service, Washington, D.C., USA

- The V&A Picture Library of The Victoria and Albert Museum, South Kensington, London, UK

- Very special thanks to Pamela Wooley, Pamela Wooley Collection, Laguna Niguel, California, USA. See more of her collection at www.pamelawooley.com.

INDEX

THE END